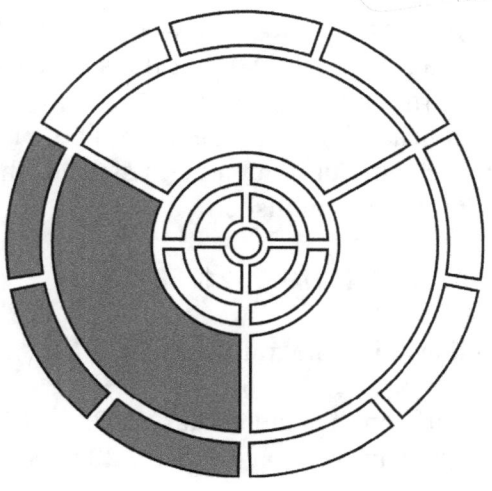

EXECUTION & PERFORMANCE

How the Most Successful Leaders Close Employee
Performance Gaps, Maintain Accountability and High
Productivity and Consistently Deliver Exceptional
Results

Brett Thomas

First Print Edition, February 2025

Copyright © 2023 Brett Thomas and Integral Publishing, LLC

No part of this publication may be reproduced, stored in a retrieval system, or transmitted in any form or by any means, electronic, mechanical, photocopying, recording, or otherwise, without written permission of the publisher.

ISBN 9798312175912

Published by Integral Publishing, LLC

First published February 2023
First print version February 2025

CONTENTS

INTRODUCTION 1

CHAPTER 1: WHY MOST LEADERSHIP DEVELOPMENT EFFORTS FAIL 3

CHAPTER 2: THE LEADERSHIP ROSETTA STONE 19

CHAPTER 3: THE UNIVERSAL LEADERSHIP MODEL 33

CHAPTER 4: THE ACCELERATING LEADERSHIP METHODOLOGY 53

CHAPTER 5: BENCHMARKING EXECUTION & PERFORMANCE LEADERSHIP CAPACITY 117

CHAPTER 6: PERFORMANCE MANAGEMENT 125

CHAPTER 7: IMPLEMENTATION 159

CHAPTER 8: PRODUCTIVITY 185

CONCLUSION: WHERE TO GO FROM HERE ON YOUR LEADERSHIP JOURNEY 219

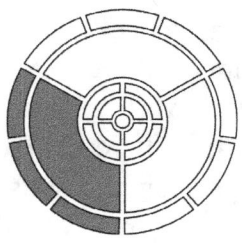

INTRODUCTION

This book introduces you to a major breakthrough in the field of leadership and leadership development. In a field where most so-called "experts" cannot even agree on a single definition of leadership, and the vast majority of leadership development programs fail, many of my clients and readers appreciate the clarity that this *Integral Leadership* book series brings to a confusing and often overwhelming topic.

Execution & Performance is the next groundbreaking book on rapid leadership development in the *Integral* Leadership book series. This book provides detailed practices, techniques and leadership skills that help managers and executives identify and close employee performance gaps, maintain accountability and high productivity on teams, and consistently deliver exceptional organizational results quarter after quarter, year after year.

Unlike most books on leadership that focus on abstract concepts and vague "leadership qualities," this book drills right down into specific, tangible techniques that amount to the exact behaviors that make leaders successful in this crucial dimension of leadership.

This book also presents a compelling argument as to why the "bogus" leadership development industry is not truly developing leaders. It introduces the world's first "Unifying Theory of Leadership" and reveals my 20-year "trade secret" on how we consistently achieve outstanding results with our leadership training in an industry where as much as 80 cents of every dollar is often wasted (according to McKinsey and others).

> *The approach to leadership and leadership development outlined in this book is almost certainly unlike anything you've ever seen before. Most leadership trainings and many books about leadership fail to define the specific abilities, skill sets, techniques and behaviors that make up the complex skill called leadership. In fact, most so-called leadership experts don't even recognize that leadership is a complex skill.*

This book is the remedy for that. The information contained within is based on over 20 years of experience advising leaders, training leaders, and coaching leaders and executive teams.

My experience avails me a unique perspective about which methods actually produce improvements in leadership skills, as opposed to those that only increase a leader's knowledge of concepts but do little to change their behavior.

I am approaching this book as a conversation with you, the reader. I am assuming that in your role of leader, you already are familiar with many aspects of leadership (and leadership development).

If you find this "conversation" valuable, I hope we can continue the conversation in my other books that unpack and expand upon the ideas introduced here. I expect that this will be one of the most valuable books you've ever read on leadership and certainly in the realm of "operational leadership."

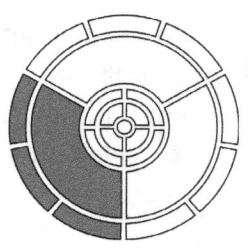

CHAPTER 1: WHY MOST LEADERSHIP DEVELOPMENT EFFORTS FAIL

Many studies from best-in-class organizations, institutions and publications in recent years have drawn the same conclusion: most leadership development efforts fail. This is no exaggeration, this is simply a matter of fact that is easily verified. Numerous studies from prominent institutions (including McKinsey and Harvard) estimate that as much as 80 cents of every dollar spent on leadership development is wasted. I have personally reviewed numerous studies that back up this assertion. This also closely aligns with my two decades of experience training and coaching leaders, as well as reviewing leadership development programs and interviewing facilitators and participants who have gone through typical leadership development programs. I have devoted my professional career to this field of leadership development and it has been of great interest to me to stay on top of the current industry practices and compare my unique methodology to what my peers and competitors are doing. I am very familiar with how leadership training and coaching is typically done (and how it is very slowly evolving).

Most leadership training programs amount to one and two week classroom seminars with lectures about leadership character traits, leader qualities, or abstract concepts that have little bearing on learning the actual concrete techniques (behaviors) that can improve leadership performance.

I'm sure you have come into contact with this problem. When you try to read books, attend leadership seminars or speak to executive coaches, it seems that they all have a different idea of what constitutes effective leadership, and their ideas largely contradict each other.

Bernard Bass, the well-respected leadership researcher and author of *The Bass Handbook of Leadership: Theory and Managerial Applications,* has noted, "Any two-day conference on leadership begins with one day of argumentation about what leadership means."

Many business professors, when speaking candidly, admit this fact that no one can agree on a definition or description of effective leadership. MIT Sloan management professor John Van Maanen has stated, "Even today, three-plus decades in, there's no real definition of it."

William Deresiewicz, the author of the book, *Excellent Sheep,* points out while every college in the country claims to be producing leaders, no one appears to know what the word even means. "There seem to be two possibilities," he writes, "The first is that it means nothing at all, or whatever definition is useful at any given time. The second is that it simply means being in charge."

Another well-known theorist, Fred Fiedler, observed, "There are almost as many definitions of leadership as there are leadership theories—and there are almost as many theories of leadership as there are psychologists working in the field."

The reason why there is almost no agreement among leadership advice givers on a single definition of "effective leadership" is that each different "type" of follower and leadership advice giver looks for different qualities and behaviors in what they consider to be "effective leaders".

This is because all followers and all advice-givers have one of our different worldviews. I will introduce these worldviews as a central part of my model in later chapters.

Here, I will mention that leadership advice is often bogus because instead of *one* definition of effective leadership, there are actually *four* definitions. Each of the four camps of advice givers has its own definition of effective leadership, which essentially amounts to them using their definition of "effective leadership" to push their own unconscious bias. The field of leadership theory and leadership development is riddled with unconscious bias and represents one of the biggest reasons so much of it is so bogus.

Few, if any, contextualize their definition of effective leadership by saying, this is a definition of effective leadership for "traditional types" or for "postmodern" or "progressive" types. Rather, they just push their unconscious bias and suggest their definition of effective leadership (for one of the worldviews) as the most effective way to lead all four types of followers. This is, of course, untrue, but that doesn't stop them from saying it.
It is no exaggeration to say that the advice givers in the leadership industry have failed to provide a definition or description of effective leadership that they can agree to.

Barbara Kellerman, a Harvard professor, takes it one step further when she says the leadership industry has failed. She explains, "The leadership industry has failed over its roughly 40 year history to improve the human condition in any major, meaningful, measurable way."

She is one of the few honest leadership professors who doesn't pull punches. Kellerman is a distinguished professor at Harvard University's John F. Kennedy School of Government. She was the Founding Executive Director at Harvard's Kennedy School's Center for Public Leadership, and previously served as the Director of the Center for the Advanced Study of Leadership at the Academy of Leadership at the University of Maryland. Kellerman has written a series of books that amount to scathing take downs of the bogus leadership industry including: *Bad Leadership, The End of Leadership,* and *Professionalizing Leadership.*

In *The End of Leadership,* she describes how despite the countless leadership programs, courses, seminars, trainers, consultants and coaches claiming to teach people how to lead, there is "scant evidence" that this enormous investment of time and money has paid off. (The leadership development industry is estimated to be $15 billion annually in the U.S. and $50 billion worldwide.)

In her follow up book, *Professionalizing Leadership,* she notes that since the publishing of the End of Leadership in 2012, she is no longer alone in beginning to blow the whistle on these unethical practices such as trying to teach a complex and technical skill in a two-week seminar (which is what most of them do). "Since then, I have been joined by a small but fierce cadre of others who point to the yawning gap between what the leadership industry claims to do, and what it does."

Kellerman is joined by Stanford's Jeffrey Pfeffer as respected academics, thoughtful intellectuals, and true insiders who have recently turned leadership industry "whistleblowers."

Pfeffer, a prominent Stanford business school professor, and author of numerous books on management and leadership, including *Leadership BS: Fixing Workplaces and Careers One Truth at a Time,* writes "The single biggest barrier to effective leadership is, in my view, the leadership industry itself. Instead of telling people the skills and behaviors they need to be effective in getting things done, we tell them almost the opposite– blandishments about how we wish people would be, and how we wish workplaces were."

He states flatly "The leadership industry has failed. It's not just that all the efforts to develop better leaders have failed to appreciably improve leadership, but they often make things much worse."

Pfeffer writes, "If one is at all sensitive to the human costs incurred as leaders flame out and lose their jobs, cares and concerns that I and I suspect many others share, then the continuing failure of the leadership industry in all of its forms and activities to make things better needs to be both explained and remedied."

Finally, leadership researcher and New York Times bestselling author Duff McDonald describes the leadership industry this way, "Most of it is bullshit. Unfortunately, there are few business school faculty who could ever summon the courage to admit such a thing. But some do, and using the same language."

For our purposes here, I want to highlight three crucial facts in this whole sordid affair that is the leadership training and coaching industry.

First, the vast majority of so-called leadership experts, trainers and coaches do not know the answers to the most basic questions about leadership: what is leadership, how does it work, and how can you develop it?

Second, as I explained above, none of the leadership experts can agree on which approach or style works best. In fact, about 90% of experts will tell you that the style they advocate is the "best" style and should pretty much be used with all people and circumstances.

Finally, as I mentioned already and will explain in more detail later in this book, the reason that the experts can't agree on the above fundamentals is because they are "subject to their own worldview bias." I will explain this in more detail later, but this essentially, it means that they are unaware of their assumptions and biases about human psychology, human motivation, and follower's needs and behavior.

My colleagues and I, under the guidance of my mentor Ken Wilber, were the first to notice (and teach and write about) this pattern. This pattern, definitively explains why there are so many definitions and descriptions of "effective" leadership that wildly contradict each other to the point of being often mutually exclusive.

This is why, as you will see shortly, worldviews are right at the center of my model. And the different leadership approaches (or styles as they can be called) that each of the four worldviews expects from legitimate and credible leaders (in their eyes) is also at the center of my model. This is what makes it universal.

Rather than a one-size-fits-all approach that amounts to pushing one's unconscious worldview bias, the new approach described in this book accounts for different follower worldviews, needs and preferences, and accounts for the four universal leadership styles seen in nearly all leadership theory literature and leadership research.

My "Universal Leadership Model," explained in detail in a later chapter, is the first model that connects these four universal worldviews with the four universal leadership styles. This connection forms the heart of the "Unifying Theory of Leadership" that I developed with Ken Wilber at the Integral Institute.

This "meta theory" of leadership explains which leadership approach (or style) will work with which people and circumstances, and what approaches will be disastrous with which people and circumstances.

My *Practice-based Leadership Development* methodology, which I will explain in detail in a later chapter, is also unique in that it is the first to break down the technical and complex skill of leadership into three "essential abilities" and nine essential leadership practices, and then proceeds to train leaders using "Deliberate Practice" which comes from the field of Expert Performance Theory, developed by Anders Ericsson.

In the next chapter, *The Leadership Rosetta Stone,* I outline the four different definitions of "effective leadership" that the four different camps of leadership advice- givers offer (which reflect their unconscious worldview bias).

For now, it is useful to offer a stripped down, you could say generic or "worldview agnostic" definition, free of worldview bias.

> *Leadership: the ability or activity of inspiring and/or influencing people in relationship, over time, toward shared goals.*

The word "leadership" implies a trust-based relationship over time with shared goals, and the word "follower" implies voluntary (consensual) participation. Remember that followership is voluntary. A follower chooses to see a person as their leader, and that can be revoked (by the follower) at any time. A follower offers discretionary effort, that is effort above and beyond what would be considered compliance, in the case of an authority figure compelling them to comply with their order.

So when influence occurs within the context of a leader-follower relationship, the follower is voluntarily participating in being influenced. Put another way, followers actually want the leader to influence them. Followers give the leader consent to influence them.

Bringing all of this together, we can think of "leadership influence" as *affecting a follower in such a way that they voluntarily change how they think or behave.*

The next big idea I want to highlight in this introduction lies at the very heart of why 80% of leadership development efforts fail, and why so much of leadership theory and so much leadership advice, is so utterly bogus.

This may strike you as a little bit provocative, controversial, or, in the worst case even condescending. But it's really none of those things if you hear me out and grasp the nuance of the reality that I'm pointing out for you.

So, bear with me and you will be glad that you did. Many leadership trainers and coaches talk about leadership as if it is about personality traits, or qualities, or vague concepts like EQ (more on this later). While these topics are interesting in the background, discussing them does next to nothing to help leaders actually improve their leadership performance.

Many leadership trainers and coaches talk about leadership as if it is about personality traits, or qualities or vague concepts like EQ (more on this later). While these topics are interesting in the background, discussing them does next to nothing to help leaders actually improve their leadership performance. Improving leadership performance has little to do with concepts and everything to do with skill. The vast majority of leadership trainers and coaches seem to be ignorant of the relatively obvious and definitely indisputable fact that leadership is a technical and complex skill.

> *There is only one way to learn a technical and / or complex skill. That is to train in the specific, requisite techniques until they are internalized as habits, then layer on more techniques to create skills, then combine several new skills to create new "skill sets" and ultimately those skill sets mature into what we call "abilities."*

This crucial point is a central element in my rapid leadership development methodology called "Accelerating Leadership," that is the subject of Chapter 4. To get better at leadership, you must understand the nature of leadership. Leadership is not a set of personality traits and it is not some vague concept (although many authors, trainers and coaches speak about it as though it is).

> *Leadership is a technical and complex skill, no different from all the many other technical and complex skills you have already learned both as a child and as an adult.*

You know this intuitively, but for some odd reason, most leadership authors, trainers and coaches don't seem to.

Learning the technical and complex skill of leadership is no different than learning any of those other technical and complex skills that you already taken the time to learn. The method is exactly the same. Yet less than 10% of leadership development programs use it.

Learning leadership is exactly the same as learning to play a musical instrument, mastering a martial art or sport, flying an airplane or any other technical and/or complex skill. How could it be otherwise?

To "reinvent leadership" we must first face the stark reality that leadership, like every other technical and complex skill we have already learned in our lives, is comprised of skills and those skills are, in turn, comprised of techniques (that can also be referred to as "practices").

Any proposed explanation of leadership that fails to point to the techniques and practices that comprise the technical and complex skill called "leadership" is flawed from the start. And this is why about 90% of models, frameworks and explanations offered by leadership advice-givers are bogus.

This is such an important point, I am going to revisit it several times in this book coming at it from a variety of different angles and using different analogies. Please pardon my deliberate repetition, but if there is one thing you must understand, it is this. And I don't want you to just be familiar with it as a concept, I want you to believe it and understand it in your bones. Once you do, all of your future leadership development efforts (and the efforts in your organization) will be much easier and more effective. This is one of the main things I want you to get out of this book.

Let me illustrate this crucial point in very concrete terms that I hope you can relate to on a personal level. I will refer to several other common technical and complex skills that you may have already learned.

Learning Guitar

No one in their right mind would try to learn to play an instrument, try to learn a martial art, or try to learn to fly an airplane the way 90% of leadership development programs train leadership. Can you imagine trying to learn to play the guitar by reading case studies of great guitar players in history, or worse, hearing stories about the accomplishments of great guitarists, or worse still, reading a list of character traits of these men and women?

Learning a Martial Art

Can you imagine trying to learn Kung Fu by hearing stories about Bruce Lee, and descriptions of his personality traits or by merely adopting his mindset or philosophy?

As absurd as this sounds, it is even more absurd that this is exactly what approximately 90% of leadership development programs are doing in the $15 billion-a-year leadership development industry (in the United States alone).

My team and I have been creating and delivering successful leadership development programs for over two decades, and I am now calling out these bogus industry practices. Research shows clearly that programs that emphasize leadership qualities, traits, philosophy, and case studies (instead of techniques and practices) fail to help leaders improve their leadership skills or their leadership performance.

Learning Piano

I want you to pause for a moment and imagine signing up your son or daughter to a training to learn to play piano and asking them what techniques your child will be practicing each week. Now imagine that their answer is, "Our students don't practice any specific techniques. Our students study the stories and personality traits of great piano players."

There is an entire field called "Complex Skill Instructional Design." Google it.

It is a very well-known fact in training and development that in order to learn any technical or complex skill, you must break the overall ability down into specific skill sets and skills, and then down to the techniques that make up those skills.

This is common sense. You already know this.

Sports Such as Baseball or Basketball

Consider the technical and complex skill called baseball. Many children learn this complex skill. Perhaps you did. When you (or your child, niece or nephew) learned the ability to play baseball, it was broken down to *throwing, catching, hitting the ball, and running the bases.* In the case of basketball, it is *dribbling, passing, shooting* and *rebounding.* In the case of mixed martial arts, it is *wrestling, kick-boxing* and *grappling.*

There is also a well-known field called "Expert Performance Theory" or "Deliberate Practice" (as it is better known). You have no doubt heard of "10,000 hours" as the estimated amount of time it takes for a person practicing deliberately to go from beginner to expert level in any complex skill.

Why don't leadership development programs incorporate "Deliberate Practice" into their efforts and teach their students the practices (the techniques and skills) that leaders need to be effective?

My partners, colleagues and I have been teaching the complex skill called "leadership" using "complex skill instructional design" and "deliberate practice" for more than 20 years. I have logged more than 20,000 hours doing precisely that. So, let me save you a lot of time, energy, money and heartburn and tell you what does not work and exactly what does actually work for leadership development.

I summarize what works in this introduction and will unpack each of these ideas in different chapters within the book.

Leadership, like any other complex skill, is made up of a specific set of skills with discrete, concrete behaviors that can be practiced, repeated, and internalized as habits.

Again, using baseball as a familiar example, you have to be able to throw, hit, run, and do several other skills before you have the ability that we call "baseball." The same goes for martial arts, music, flying an airplane and leadership.

> *There is only one way to learn a complex skill: practice and internalize a technique, then combine several techniques (in layers) over time.*

This is called "complex skill instructional design" and "deliberate practice." It involves breaking the broader ability down into smaller skill sets and skills, then teaching those specific techniques and behaviors.

Clearly, to learn (or improve) this ability called leadership, it must be broken down into specific skill sets and discrete techniques (behaviors).

Think about mixed martial arts (MMA). There are three major abilities (*wrestling, striking* and *grappling*) and each is made up of a dozen or so techniques. The fact that MMA athletes have separate training and separate coaches for wrestling, striking and grappling underscores the nature of this complex ability (which has many parallels to leadership, which is obviously at least as complex as martial arts).

I will now summarize why I think the leadership development industry is not developing leaders.

1. Most leadership trainers and coaches do not recognize leadership as a technical and complex skill, and instead, speak about leader character traits (or qualities as they often call them).

2. Most leadership trainers and coaches focus primarily or even exclusively on the leader and under-emphasize or completely

ignore the leadership context (the specific circumstances that will call for different approaches).

3. Most leadership trainers and coaches under-emphasize or completely ignore the followers, their worldviews (values, beliefs, assumptions), their specific needs, and their preferences for the kind of leadership they will resonate with

4. Most leadership advice-givers make "one-size-fits-all" pronouncements that this is the "best way" to lead with all followers in all circumstances. Any leadership advice that fails to provide guidelines for which people and circumstances this method will work with is bad advice because no leadership approach will work with all follower types and in all circumstances.

I can summarize all of this by saying that the vast majority of so-called "leadership experts" in today's leadership development industry do not know what leadership actually is, can't explain to customers how leadership actually works, and certainly do not understand how to develop this complex and technical skill (that they don't even recognize as such).

I will reserve an in-depth analysis of what is badly wrong with the leadership development industry for my book, *Blowing the Whistle on Bogus Leadership: Veteran Industry Insider Reveals Why the Leadership Development Industry is Not Developing Leaders.*

Now that we have discussed what makes so much leadership advice bogus, we will transition into a description of a series of astonishing breakthroughs that have occurred in recent years that will allow us to actually reinvent leadership in the coming years.

The beginning of these breakthroughs occurred in the early 2000s at the Stagen Leadership Academy that I co-founded and at Ken Wilber's Integral Institute (where I was the head of the Business and Leadership Center). It would be impossible to reinvent leadership without an "integral" understanding of the topic, because only an "integral" approach would bring the necessary complexity and nuance to recognize the different paradigms, follower worldviews, dimensions (Integral theory calls "quadrants") and the developmental nature of leadership ability. This "integral" view of leadership is the focus of the next chapter.

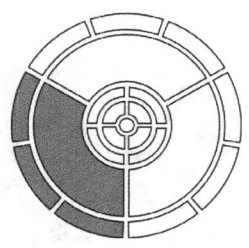

CHAPTER 2: THE LEADERSHIP ROSETTA STONE

The Rosetta Stone is an ancient Egyptian artifact on which the same information is inscribed in: Egyptian hieroglyphs, Demotic, and Greek. The discovery of the Rosetta Stone allowed researchers to decode the language of Egyptian hieroglyphs for the first time in history. This term "Rosetta Stone" is often used idiomatically to describe any critical key that unlocks something previously difficult (or impossible) to decipher. After reviewing hundreds of leadership texts, including most of the popular books on leadership theory and practice, an unmistakable pattern emerged for me and my research team at The Integral Institute (under the mentorship of Ken Wilber) and the Stagen Leadership Academy. Nearly all "leadership theory" texts and books that claim to explain the "best" way to lead describe the writers' subjective ideas about which leadership tactics work best with followers based on their own assumptions about the world and the people being led. All of the texts that described the authors' opinions about which leadership techniques/approaches work best with followers are based on their assumptions about the world and the people being led.

With rare exceptions, the authors' inherent assumptions about the world and people (and biases for which approaches should be used) lined up with the four "worldviews" I had learned about from Ken Wilber, Jean Gebser, Robert Kegan and the other developmental psychologists I had studied or worked with.

This turned out to be the key to unlocking the Universal Theory of Leadership. When we group the leadership theories, approaches, techniques and tools by the worldview of their advocate, we see that in most cases, those methods do work well for followers who share that worldview. Integral theory provides us with an easy way (if you know what to look for) to identify follower mindsets, or worldviews.

Therefore, if we know a follower's worldview, we will know with a great deal of accuracy which leadership styles and approaches will be most resonant with them, that they will feel drawn to, will trust, willingly follow, and the leader for whom they will happily offer their "discretionary effort."

Next, I will first summarize the four most common worldviews most relevant in organizational life in the developed world and briefly introduce the four universal leadership styles and show how you apply them to the three essential leadership abilities and nine leadership core competencies.

The Four Universal Worldviews

In a later section of this book entitled "Values Research," I will provide a detailed description of decades of values and worldviews research that demonstrates that nearly all major theorists (who study values and worldviews) agree that there are four universal worldviews, and nearly all also agree on their common names). For now, I will keep the discussion brief and simply introduce the Four Universal Worldviews that are essential building blocks for our Leadership Rosetta Stone.

These four worldviews should be familiar to you by now as I introduced them previously when I explained the four leadership paradigms.

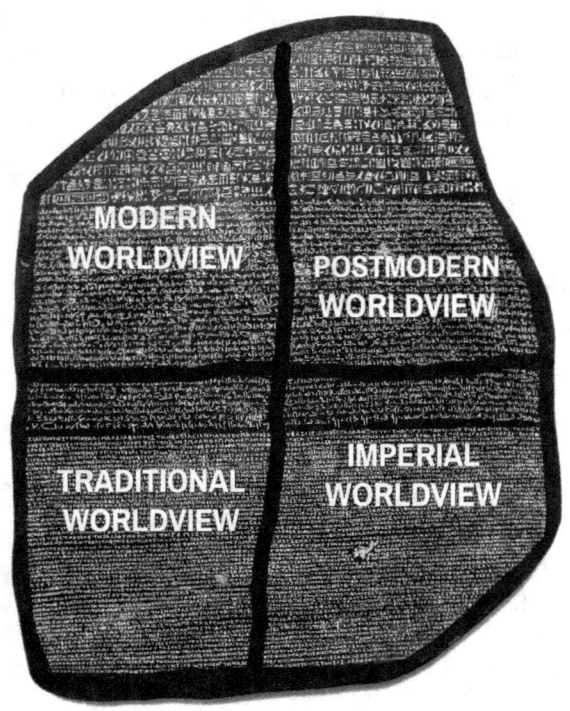

The Imperial Worldview

The Imperial worldview first emerged in society during the time of feudal kingdoms and is roughly equivalent to the Bronze Age and is still very much alive and well today. People with this worldview see the world as made up of "predators and prey", where the strongest and most cunning survive, gain power, and satisfy their wants. They tend to be fiercely independent living by their "own rules" and are disinterested in conforming to many social norms, are driven to break free from limits, achieve their goals, or impose their will. People with this worldview tend to believe the best way to think and behave is "my way." People with an *Imperial* worldview find the *Autocratic* leadership style most credible.

The Traditional Worldview

The Traditional worldview initially emerged historically with the monotheistic religious traditions and the Roman Empire, and we see it starting with the Iron Age (and continuing through the Middle Ages.) People with this worldview see the world as an ordered existence under the control of a higher authority and ultimate truth. They tend to see the world in a concrete, literal, and dualistic manner: right vs. wrong, good vs. evil, and so on. They emphasize social stability and "mainstream" morality. People with this worldview tend to believe that there is only one right way to think and behave. People with a *Traditional* worldview will find the *Authority* style most credible.

The Modern Worldview

The Modern Age emerged during the historical western enlightenment and the dawn of scientific thinking we associate with "The Renaissance", which eventually led to the Industrial Age. People with this worldview tend to believe in the advancement of humankind through the application of the rational mind and its scientific, technological, and medical manifestations. Life is to be met and mastered by finding the best way to act on its limitless opportunities. People with this worldview tend to believe that while there are many valid ways to think and behave, there is always one best way. People with *Modern* worldview will find the *Strategic* leadership style most credible.

The Postmodern Worldview

The Postmodern worldview first emerged in the 1960s with the advent of computer technology, networking and globalization and we associate it with the Information Age. People with this worldview believe the world is a diverse web of interrelationships where life forms depend on each other for survival, and there is no single explanatory system (view of reality) that can account for all the phenomena of life; rather there are many truths. People with this worldview tend to believe that there are many valid ways to think and behave but that there is no real way to judge the superiority of one way or another. People with *Postmodern* worldview will find the *Humanistic* leadership style most credible.

Now that we have initially defined the four worldviews, we will look at the four "universal leadership styles" that must be paired with people who share these corresponding worldviews in order to be viewed as a credible leader in the eyes of your followers.

The Four Universal Leadership Styles

To aid in the learning process, I will first provide a "fly over" with the four very brief definitions and descriptions of the four universal leadership styles that provide a hub that the Universal Leadership Model spins around.

Autocratic Leadership: The person with the most power leads via command and control. In short, this leadership style is based on power and control.

Authority Leadership: The person with positional authority leads via chain of command. In short, this leadership style is based on rules and compliance.

Strategic Leadership: The person with the most expertise leads via strategic planning and tangible incentives. In short, this leadership style is based on expertise and winning.

Humanistic Leadership: Leadership is not vested in any one person; rather, it emerges from the inclusive collective via consensus in the service of the greater good. In short, this leadership style is based on equality and consensus.

Now that you have a basic idea of what these four styles are, I will elaborate on the simple definitions and add a more detailed description of each style.

Autocratic Leadership

Simple definition: *The person with the most power leads via command and control.*

Approach: This style reflects a "Unilateral" approach to leadership. When using this style, leaders impose their will through reputation, fear and respect, tightly control information and choices, reward compliance and punish disloyalty. The oldest of the styles, is the way you would expect a ruler (such as a king or dictator) to "rule" their subjects. It is still extremely popular today (both with some rules and also with a surprisingly large percentages of followers and also voters).

Appreciated by: People with predominantly Imperial worldviews who respect dominance and aggression, and who prefer to follow leaders who are perceived as being the strongest, toughest, and most dominant who will be able to protect them from (or defeat) their enemies. Another word for leaders who use this style is "strongman" leaders.

Authority Leadership

This is also known as "Authority" leadership, "chain of command" leadership, and "authoritarian" leadership.

Simple definition: *The person with positional authority leads via chain of command.*

Approach: This style reflects a "Hierarchical" approach to leadership. When using this style, leaders compel followers to dutifully comply with the established protocols, coordinate efforts and meet requirements prescribed by authority. This style is the most "parental" of all the styles; the leader is in a position of "parent" and followers are in the position of "child."

Appreciated by: People with Traditional worldviews who value honor, service, loyalty, and conformity, and share traditional beliefs and a willingness to sacrifice now for future rewards... and who prefer to follow leaders who are perceived as having positional and/or moral authority.

Strategic Leadership

This is also known as "Expert Leadership." Some academics who are strongly biased toward the next style (Humanistic) will refer to this style as "Transactional leadership."

Simple definition: *The person with the most expertise leads via strategic planning and tangible incentives.*

Approach: This style reflects a "Transactional" approach to leadership. When using this style, leaders leverage financial incentives to motivate teams to execute strategic plans in order to outperform competitors.

Appreciated by: People with a Modern worldview who seek opportunities to advance toward their individual goals and who prefer to follow leaders who are perceived as having the most expertise and ability to achieve goals.

Humanistic Leadership

This is also known as "Inclusive leadership," "Transformational Leadership," "Collaborative leadership," and "Self-Managed Teams" (the members lead themselves).

Simple definition: *Leadership is not vested in any one person; rather, it emerges from the inclusive collective via consensus in the service of the greater good.*

Approach: This style reflects a "Transformational" approach to leadership. When using this style, leaders strive for equality and inclusiveness by inviting people's feelings and intuition via dialog to arrive at consensus. This style attempts to draw out the "human potential" of their followers, and work together collaboratively toward common goals. This approach strongly favors "self-managed teams" over "single-leader led teams."

Appreciated by: People with a Postmodern worldview who value diversity, equality, inclusion, authenticity, connection, opportunity for personal growth and contribution to the collective, and who prefer to follow leaders who are perceived as being aware, sensitive to the well-being of others, who strive for consensus, and who always treats others as equals.

Pairing Leadership Styles with Follower Worldviews

Followers with an *Imperial* worldview will find Autocratic leadership credible. These followers look for a leader who is perceived to be powerful and who can protect them from and/or defeat their enemies. If you use any of the other three styles with a person with an Imperial worldview, you run the risk of undermining your credibility with these types of followers.

People with a *Traditional* worldview will find Authority leadership credible. These followers are looking for a leader who is perceived to have "moral" or positional authority (and the "morals" in this case will always be defined by traditional values and/or traditional religious beliefs. Again, if you use any of the other three styles with a person with a Traditional worldview, you run the risk of undermining your credibility because they won't see you as a legitimate leader (according to what they look for in a leader).

People with a *Modern* worldview will find Strategic leadership credible. These followers are looking for the leader to be the person with the most expertise who is most likely able to help them achieve their goals. Again, if you use any of the other three styles with a person with a Modern worldview, you run the risk of undermining your credibility as you don't exhibit the qualities (and the approaches) that they associate with credible leaders and competent leadership.

People with a *Postmodern* worldview will find Humanistic leadership credible. These followers are looking for the leader to treat everyone as an equal and who strives for equality and consensus. Again, if you use any of the other three styles with a person with a Postmodern worldview, you run the risk of undermining your credibility, as they may not see you as a legitimate leader (they might use the phrase "conscious leader").

The Theorists Are Also Subject to Their Worldviews

By now you are starting to recognize the pattern. The four universal worldviews track perfectly with the four widely acknowledged "paradigms of leadership" put forth by the different experts. As I will explain in this book, the theorists who put forth leadership theories are often subject to their own worldview biases. The advocates of the different approaches (or styles of leadership) can be seen clearly to hold these different worldviews. In most cases their bias is unconscious and they do not admit or acknowledge the existence of the other three worldviews. And they certainly don't agree that the other leadership paradigms (other than the one they are biased towards) hold any merit at all. This is of course ridiculous and reflects the fact that they are leaving out the context dimension of leadership. Perhaps most embarrassing of all, many so-called leadership experts and leadership training programs seem to leave out followers altogether! Even many of the most respected leadership authorities have overlooked this pattern that the follower's mindset (worldview) determines, in large part, which "leadership paradigm" will offer the most utility in that context.

This chapter has introduced you to Integral Leadership. This is an important topic that warrants a much longer treatment. If this interests you, see my book, *Integral Leadership: The World's First Unifying Theory of Leadership That Will Forever Transform How You Understand, Practice and Develop Leadership*

We are now ready to assemble the "Universal Leadership Model!" As a way to help you not only fully understand the model but also to appreciate the relationships between its different components, I will walk you through a logical, step-by-step process of building the model section-by-section in the next chapter.

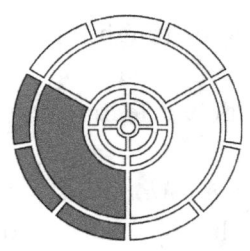

CHAPTER 3:
THE UNIVERSAL
LEADERSHIP MODEL

When we combine the "Leadership Rosetta Stone", which clearly articulates four distinct approaches to leadership, with the three "Inherent Leadership Responsibilities" and the nine "Essential Leadership Skills", you have what I call the "Universal Leadership Model." All leaders everywhere, regardless of context, share these three inherent leadership responsibilities. All leaders fulfill their responsibilities by engaging in the activities we see under each of the nine leadership skill sets (also called "core competencies").Naturally, the activities, techniques and skills may use different names, but the work of leadership is universal, and the skills leaders need to be effective are also universal. What is different from culture to culture and leader to leader is the "approach" or the "style" with which they undertake these activities. A leader can engage the activities associated with each skill set using any of the four universal leadership styles: *Autocratic, Authority, Strategic,* and *Humanistic,* which track perfectly with the four predominant leadership paradigms we explored previously.

While this may sound quite straightforward, my colleagues and I are the only ones who are approaching leadership and leadership development in this uniquely effective way.

Our *Universal Leadership Model* is an "integrally-informed" approach to leadership. In the year 2000, I created a one-year training program called "The Integral Leadership Program" and launched a leadership academy with my close friend Rand Stagen to bring this approach to the business world with the goal of helping to "make business a force for good." As of this writing, more than two thousand companies (and growing) have adopted this approach.

This "integral" or "conscious" approach to leadership played a central role in helping to launch and grow the "Conscious Capitalism" movement (also known as the "Conscious Business Movement). I mention this to highlight the fact that this is not merely a model or framework. This approach to leadership and leadership development that is not "theoretical;" rather, it is tried and proven to be extraordinarily effective over more than two decades with thousands of companies including non-profit companies and other types of organizations around the world, even in developing countries. Many people familiar with the field of leadership development believe that this approach is one of the most effective, if not the most effective approach to leadership development that exists.

In this chapter we will assemble the "Universal Leadership Model" from the components we have already introduced: 1) The Leadership Rosetta Stone, 2) Inherent Leadership Responsibilities and 3) Leadership Core Competencies. For clarity's sake, I will bring one element in at a time, illustrate each, and then combine them as we assemble the model.

First, recall the four universal leadership styles: *Strategic, Humanistic, Authority* and *Autocratic*.

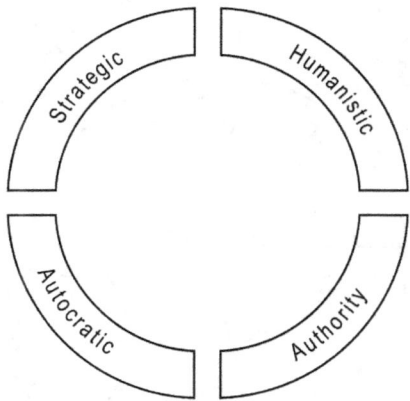

Next, the *Leadership Rosetta Stone* revealed the four predominant "follower worldviews." And we learned that each worldview has a specific definition of legitimate leadership and is looking for very different things in people who they view as credible leaders.

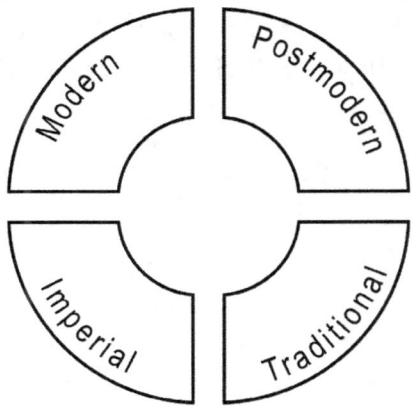

We now recognize that for leadership to be viewed as effective (by those being led), the correct leadership style must be paired with the follower's worldview (which dictates how they define effective leadership and what they look for in a credible leader. When we bring the styles and the worldviews together, we can illustrate it like this.

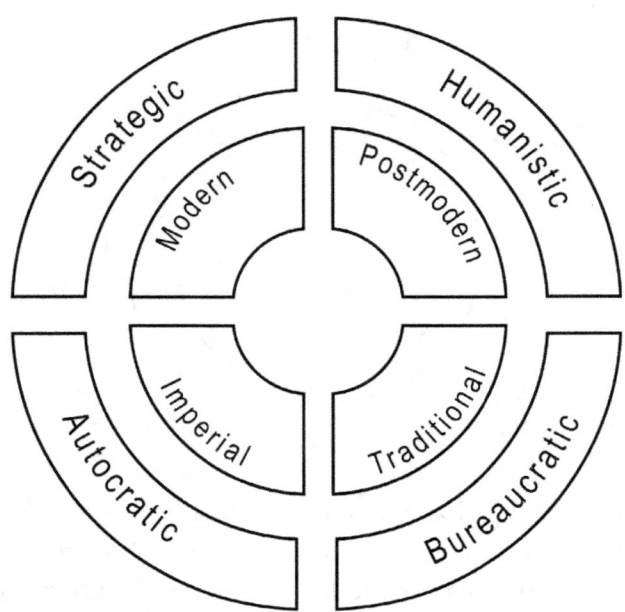

In the above illustration we can see that the correct leadership style is paired with the worldview of the follower (according to the style of leadership that follower will view as credible and legitimate).

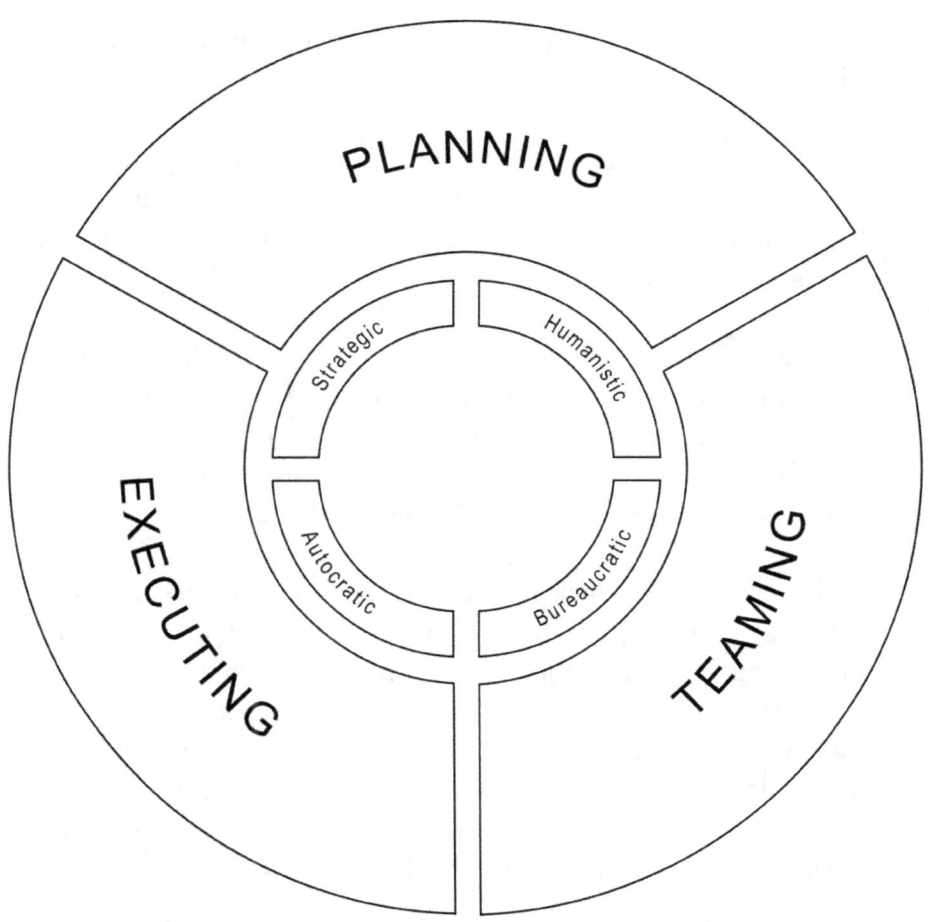

Next, you will recall that there are three "Inherent Leadership Responsibilities," which point to the three "Essential Abilities" all leaders must possess to be considered competent and adequately well-rounded leaders.

Using common terms, those are often referred to as *Planning, Teaming* and *Executing*. I introduce additional, more nuanced terms in Chapter 4: Accelerating Leadership.

When you take into account the leadership style, you can see that different types of leaders will take a different approach, that is, use a different style as they fulfill these responsibilities. Put another way, all leaders demonstrate three essential abilities, but they use different styles.

For example, one leader may use a "Humanistic" approach to *planning, teaming* and *executing*. Another leader may use an "Autocratic" approach, another a "Strategic" approach and another a "Authority" approach.

This fact is reflected in our illustration with the four different styles pictured inside the three responsibilities. While this is a static illustration, you might want to imagine the center circle (with the leadership styles) spinning around so that different styles can be deployed with different areas of responsibilities.

Sadly, some leaders lack any versatility at all, and always use their native style (example: Strategic) with all followers. The result of only using one style is that it is only resonant with those followers who have that corresponding worldview (values and beliefs). For the other estimated 25-75% of the people in typical diverse organizations (who have a different worldview), that leader's style comes across as ineffective, out of touch, lame, not trustworthy, clueless or even foolish. Imagine how ridiculous the positional, "parental," authoritarian style comes across to postmodern followers who despise hierarchy and believe that legitimate leaders always treat everyone as equals. Get it?

Versatile leaders (this includes all leaders who have had the benefit of my Integral Leadership training) develop much-needed capacity to switch their style up and emphasize different leadership styles with different people and circumstances, as the situation warrants. For example, they can adopt a more Strategic style with their modern worldview, goal-oriented, success-driven followers, and then they lean on a more Humanistic style with their postmodern worldview, progressive followers who expect to be treated as an equal (and expect their feelings and perspectives to be respected and taken into account on all major organizational decisions). And that same versatile leader will adopt a more "hierarchical" Authority approach with their Traditional worldview followers who see legitimate leaders as using their positional authority to enforce rules and compliance.

Next, you will recall that for each of the inherent leadership responsibilities, that leaders engage a variety of practices, activities, skill sets and/or "competencies" to fulfill their responsibilities. In our pragmatic framework, we describe three skill sets for each of the three responsibilities (3 skill sets x 3 responsibilities = 9 total skill sets).

Each of these nine skill sets consist of about half a dozen techniques (behaviors, not concepts). I go into much more detail about these techniques in my other books.

This next simplified illustration shows the three essential abilities (in the middle area) along with the nine skill sets around the outer ring).

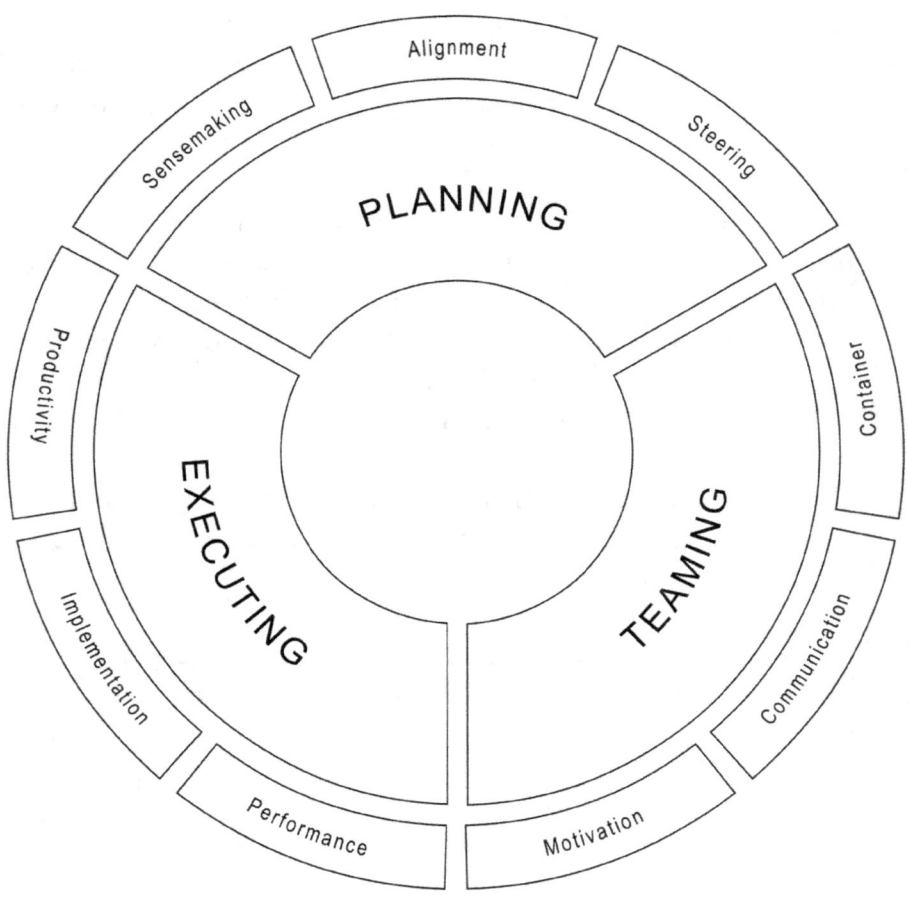

Next, we will want to bring the four leadership styles and four follower worldviews back into our illustration. This way, our illustration reflects that leaders can engage their three "essential abilities" (*planning, teaming* and *executing*) in the middle of the diagram, along with their corresponding (3x3) skill sets along the outer ring using any of these leadership styles, and those styles should be paired up correctly based on the followers being led.

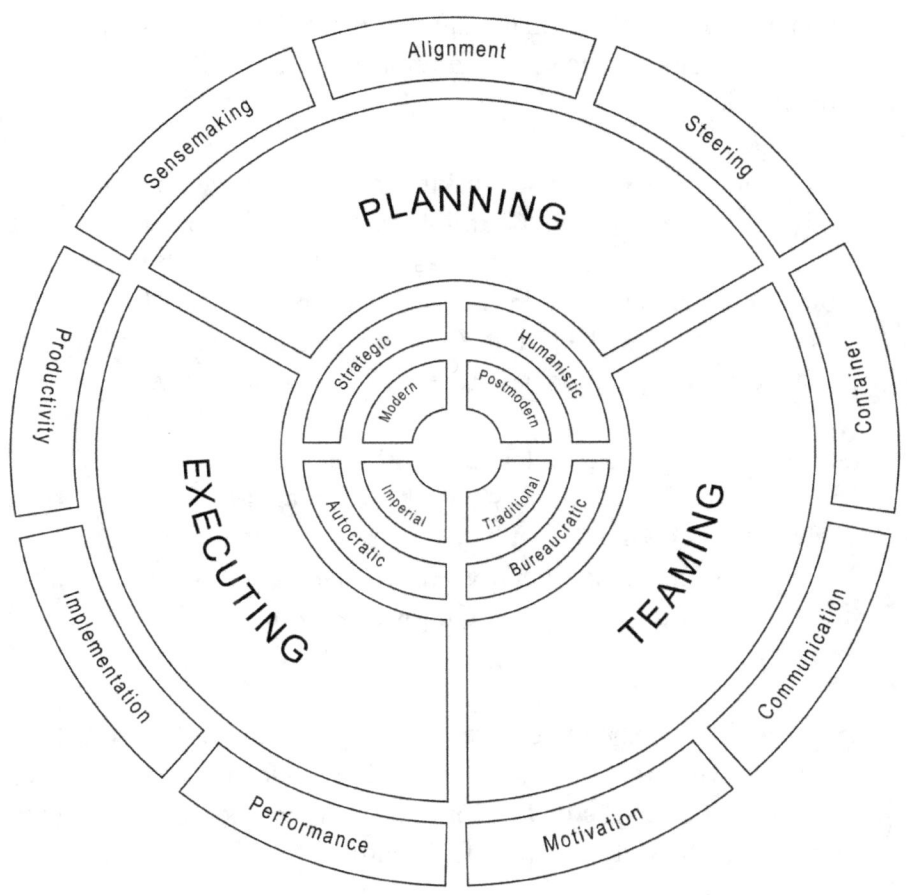

Like so. Now, this version of the model visually suggests that for each ability (middle section) and for each of the nine skill sets (outer section), there are four different styles to draw upon.

For example, there is an "authority" way to hold people accountable for job performance and a "strategic" way to hold people accountable for their performance. There is an "autocratic" approach to creating the team "container" and there is a "humanistic" approach to creating a container (and they are as different as night and day). Similarly, there is a "humanistic" way to approach alignment around vision, for example, and there is a "strategic" way to approach coming up with the vision and aligning people around it. As a final example, there is an autocratic way to motivate people and teams, an authority way, and of course a more humanistic way.

Once you have experience working with this framework, you will realize it provides a nearly unlimited amount of versatility to the art and science of leadership. Mastering this approach will enable you to be an effective leader with a diverse population of followers. Eventually you will be able to influence, motivate, inspire and guide just about anyone, regardless of their worldview.

At first, this notion of leading with the requisite versatility of shifting from "Strategic" style to the "Humanistic" or "Authority" style appears difficult. Yet, my 22 years of teaching leaders to do this shows that it is actually easier than it looks. It just takes instruction from someone who knows this framework, and a lot of practice.

Simply put, to expand your versatility, you will need to select the next style you want to master, find a role model to emulate (and/or read my other books or take one of my many courses), and then practice the new style until it feels natural.

Here is a slightly longer instruction on how to do this.

Recall that the three most common worldviews in most organizations are *Traditional, Modern* and *Postmodern*. The good news is you already have one style down, I call that one your "native style." It is likely either Strategic or Humanistic (that pairs with the Modern and Postmodern follower worldviews respectively). If your role models were highly traditional, then maybe your native style is Authority. That hierarchical style must only be used with followers with Traditional worldviews. (The other types of followers will find that "parental" approach quite off-putting, especially the postmodern types who hate hierarchy and expect legitimate leaders to treat everyone as an equal.)

Now, after you identify your "native" style, reflect on your team, organization and the followers you interact with the most.

In this example, I will assume your native style is Strategic. Well, you certainly have all the followers in your organization who have a Modern worldview covered.

What's the next largest group?

Is it Postmodern? If you work in tech or with a younger workforce (millennials and Gen Z) then you probably work with a lot of followers with the postmodern worldview. So then the "Humanistic" style is the one you want to master next!

The best way to learn that style (besides taking one of my courses) is to identify other leaders in your organization, and teachers and mentors, who are "fluent in that values dialect" and who either use the Humanistic style natively or have mastered it through practice.

Study them, notice how they always say "we" and almost never say "I". Notice how they let everyone else speak <u>first</u> before they speak. (Autocratic and Authoritarian leaders would never do that.) Pay attention to how these "Humanistic" leaders demonstrate respect for everyone's perspective, how they treat everyone as their equal, and how they strive for consensus.

Also notice the way that they hold people accountable, delegate, give feedback, motivate, handle group decisions and just about every other leader responsibility and activity is undertaken in a slightly different way than you do (contrasting the Humanistic style with the Strategic style in this hypothetical example).

The details of their Humanistic style should be obvious now that I have given you the "leadership styles cheat codes" in the form of my Leadership Rosetta Stone). The answers are all around you,

you just needed to know what to look for. And now you know exactly what to look for.

Before we move on, there are still two more elements to represent in the "Universal Leadership Model" that we have started to assemble.

Can you guess what is still missing in our illustration so far?

We have covered *followers, leadership styles, leadership responsibilities* and *leadership skills.* Recall the element that our leadership industry whistleblowers from Harvard and Stanford (Keller and Pfeffer) point out that is often ignored. Perhaps you guessed it. Recall what Lewin ignored when he studied young children doing arts and crafts to create a model of corporate leadership styles.

Did you guess it?

It is "organizational context" (or what I also call "circumstances").

Whether or not a given leader and their style (or approach) will be effective is largely a function of the context (the circumstances). As history has shown us repeatedly, an incompetent, failed, and discredited leader in one context will be heralded as a brilliant successful leader in a different context (with a different audience). Or the opposite, a leader may be very successful in one context and a dismal failure in another.

So when we add organizational context (circumstances) to our Universal Leadership Model it looks like this.

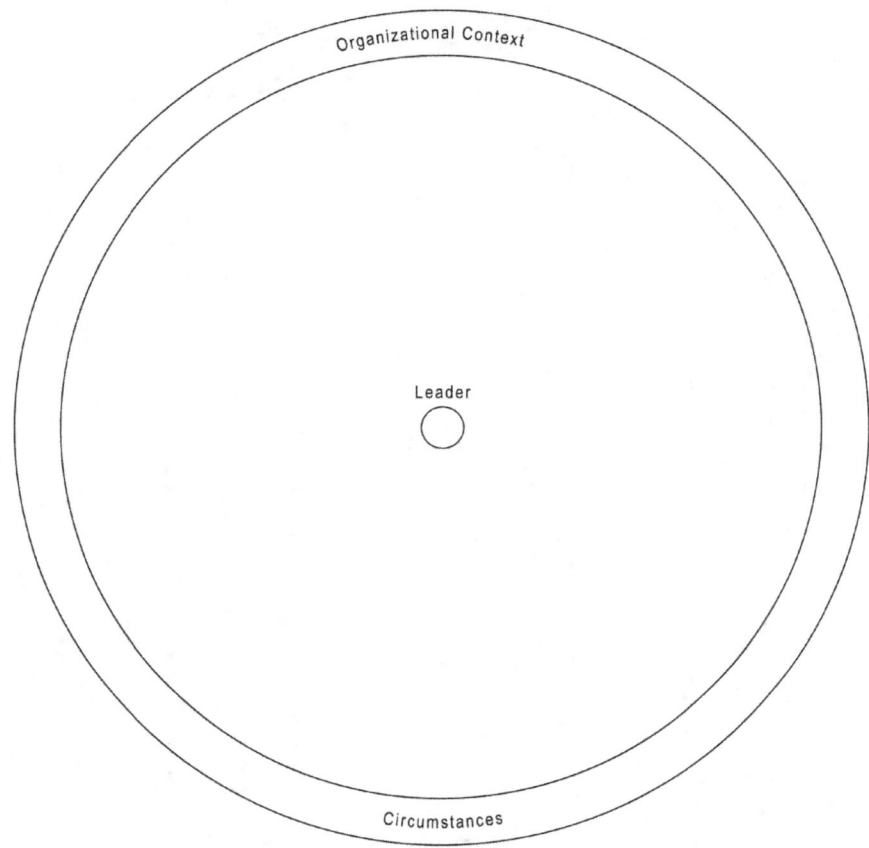

There is just one last element to add to our illustration. This last element, the leader, bears special emphasis. In this illustration you can see the leader (represented by small circle in the middle).

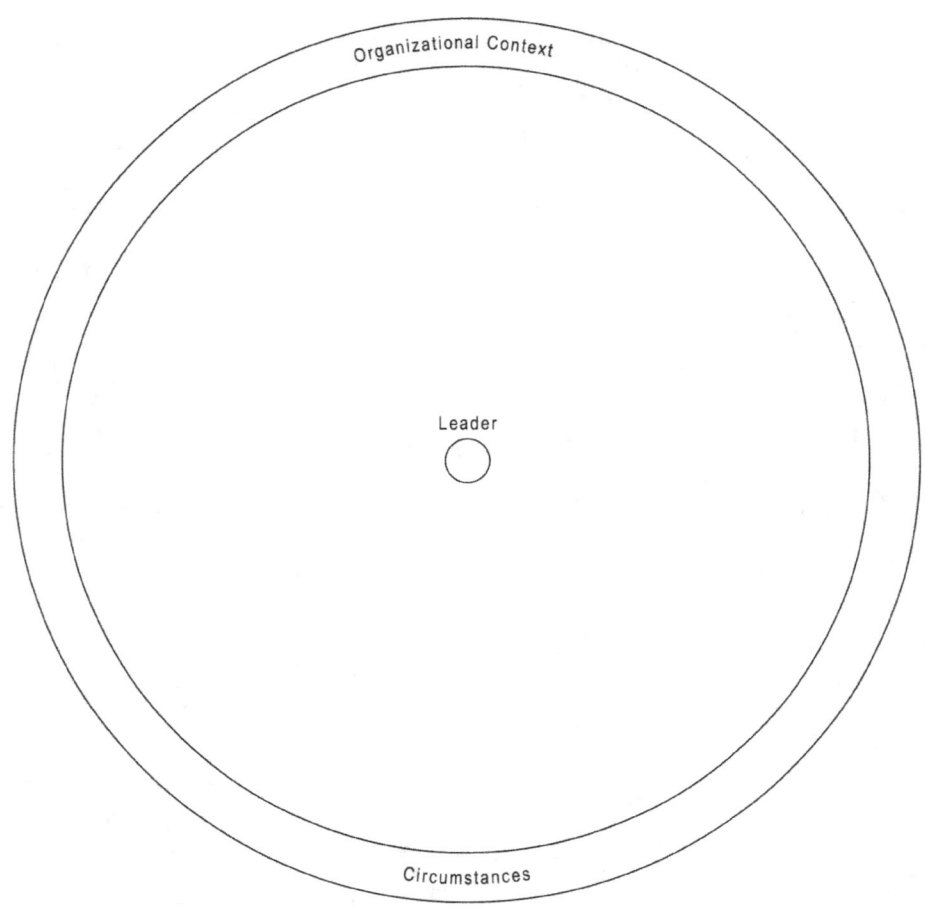

To be effective, this leader must first and foremost be able to make sense out of their circumstances. In many of our courses and coaching programs, we go into much detail about sensemaking. (You may recall it is one of the nine core competencies). Sensemaking is the leadership skill that leaders must draw upon to make sense of the context (their circumstances). In our leadership courses and coaching programs, we encourage leaders to ask the following questions:

What is really happening?
What is important?
What is needed?

And…
What is the most helpful action I can take?

If you want to read more about sensemaking, please see my book entitled, *Strategy & Alignment: How the Most Successful Leaders Analyze Needs, Prioritize, Craft Vision, Align Stakeholders and Create Smart Strategic Plans*

The next important thing for a leader to understand after understanding the organizational context, is…

Who are the followers that they wish to influence (or lead)?

The most important thing about a follower's psychological makeup is their worldview because it determines which of the four universal leadership styles they will strongly prefer (and willingly follow). The next logical piece of the Universal Leadership Model to bring in will be the followers.

The next logical piece of the Universal Leadership Model to bring in will be the <u>followers</u>."

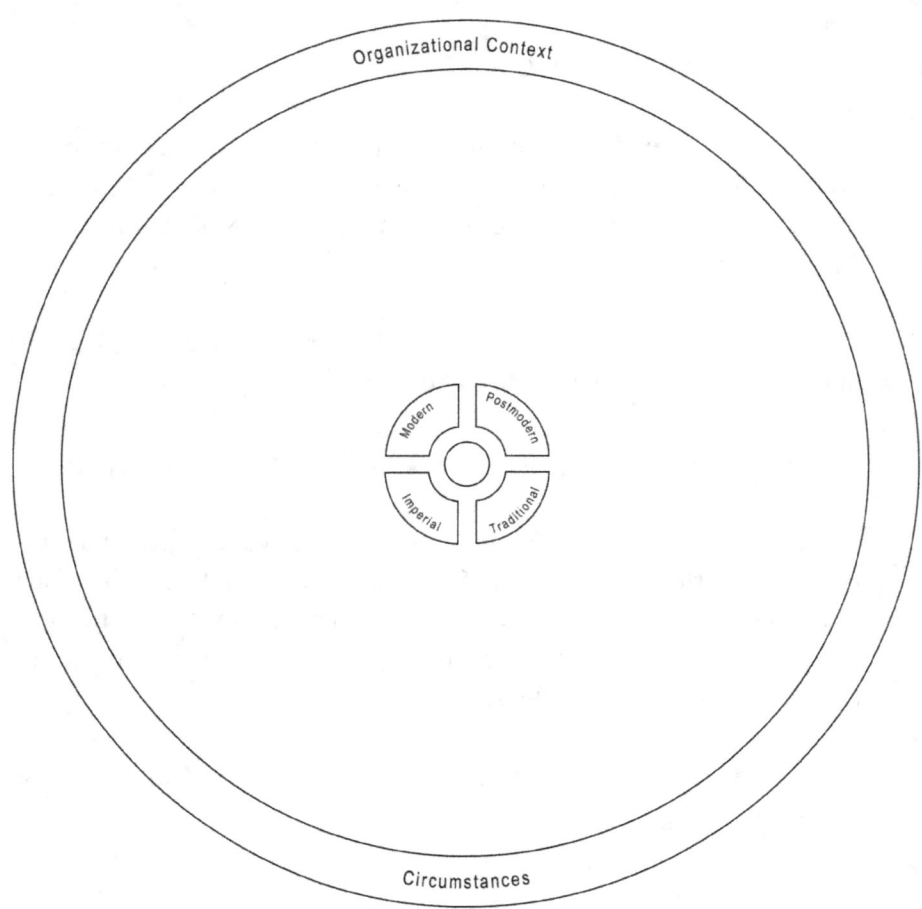

Leaders who are viewed as "credible" by followers when the leaders use the leadership style preferred by those followers (indicated in the diagram by the appropriate leadership styles being paired with follower worldviews.)

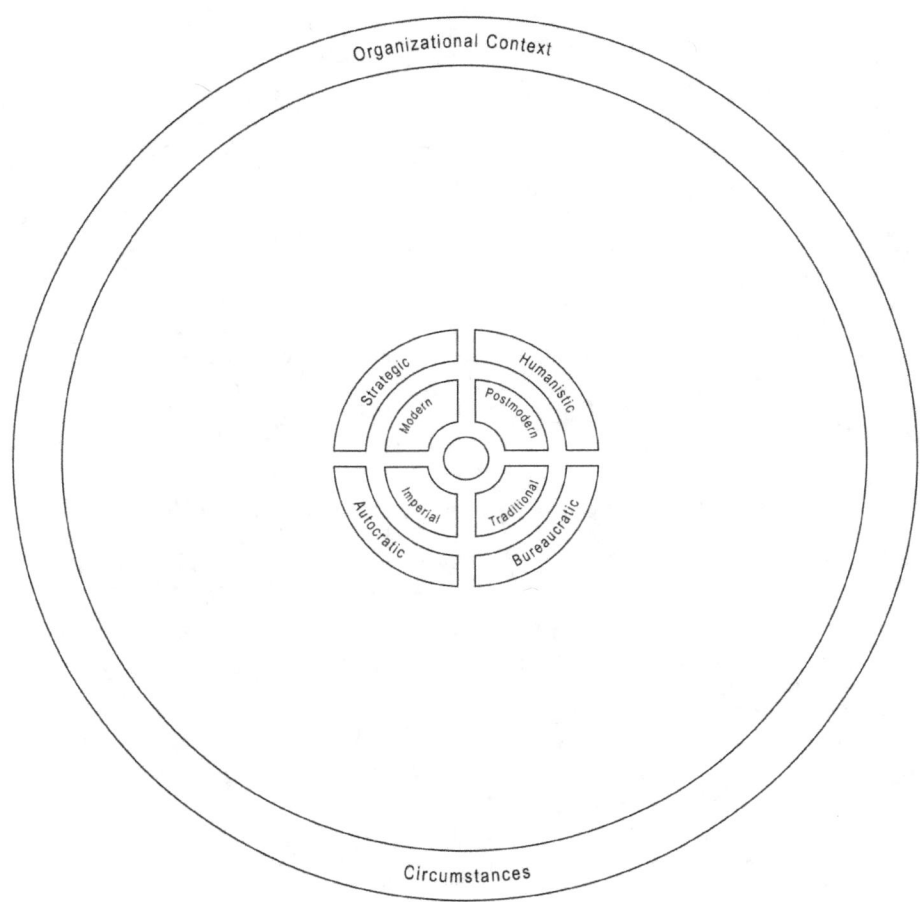

At this point, you should already know what comes next in our model. Leaders have three "inherent leadership responsibilities," also called three "essential abilities" they draw upon to fulfill their responsibilities.

The way they approach those responsibilities is a function of their "leadership style."

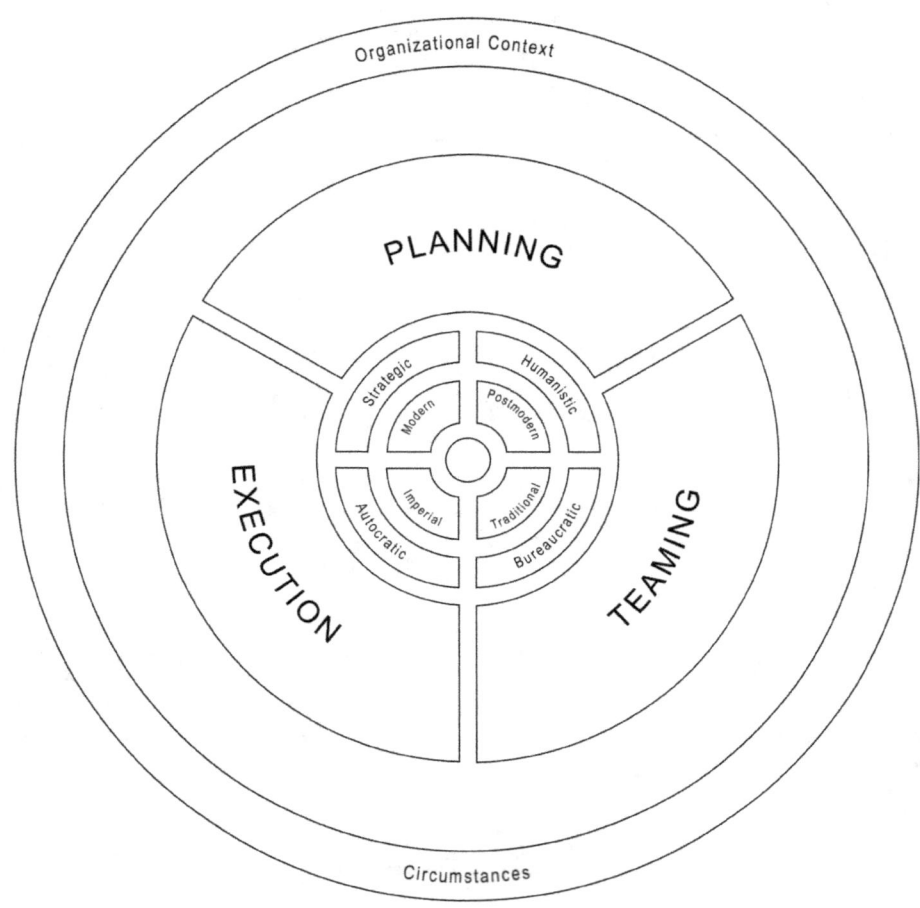

The words Planning, Teaming and Execution represent the "inherent leadership responsibilities" and also the "essential leader abilities."

Next, we know that leaders must engage in many activities, and use their "skill sets" in order to fulfill those responsibilities. Of course, each of these skill sets looks different according to the leadership style being used.

Once we bring these nine skill sets back in, we have the full Universal Leadership Model.

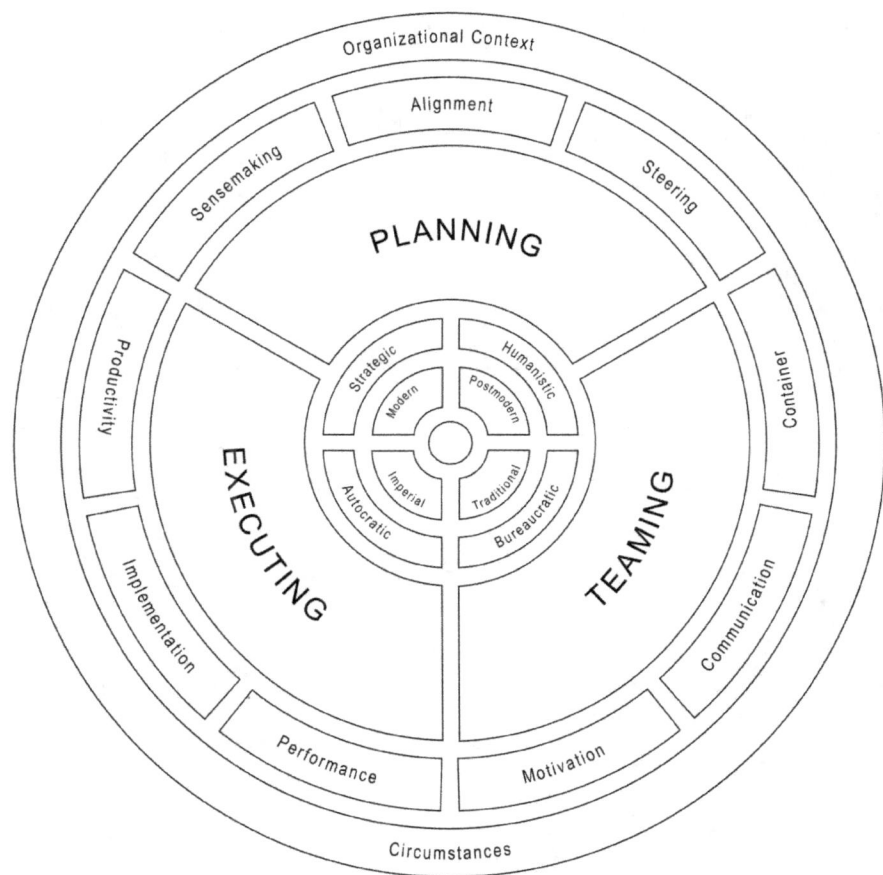

Please study this simple, yet profound, model. If you learn and apply it, it will revolutionize your leadership. This chapter provides a high-level overview of the Universal Leadership Model.

This model merits a longer discussion. If you would like to continue this discussion, with more detail and nuance, please refer to my other book, *The Universal Leadership Model: The Simplicity on the Other Side of Complexity.*

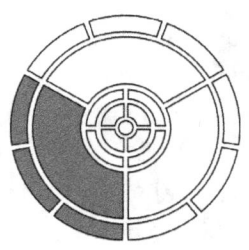

CHAPTER 4:
THE ACCELERATING LEADERSHIP METHODOLOGY

Previously, I introduced the three inherent leadership responsibilities. In this chapter, I will expand upon them to unpack the most common skill sets that leaders draw upon to fulfill those responsibilities and I will introduce the world's fastest and most effective method for improving leadership performance and organizational results. In this chapter, you will be introduced to the "practice-based leadership" approach that I invented in the early 2000s at Stagen Leadership Academy and Integral Institute. As you are about to see in this chapter, this is an absolute game changer.

As mentioned in an earlier, "character traits" or vague "leadership qualities" can't be taught or learned in any reasonable amount of time. But "technique" (also known as behavior, or practices) can absolutely be trained and learned relatively quickly. This is the key to rapid leadership development.

I'm going to be blunt again here.

Please stop listening to bogus leadership advice from the leadership industry's "snake oil salesmen" who push vague concepts like EQ, confidence, trustworthiness, or charisma.

Vague concepts have never helped a leader increase this technical and complex skill. Seek advice from people who have legitimate expertise in the requisite leadership skills and "techniques" and know how to help clients develop those skills (by teaching the requisite techniques, not vague concepts).

"What, abandon EQ" you might be saying to yourself? No, of course you don't abandon your ability for emotional intelligence.

Of course emotional intelligence is important... that is the <u>capacity</u> that we point to when we use the term emotional intelligence is important... along with *social intelligence, cognitive intelligence, moral intelligence* and so on.

I realize these intelligences are important. In fact, I have taught and written extensively about these human capacities over the last two decades. My colleagues and I have developed assessments to measure low, medium and high levels of development along these intelligences (which integral and developmental psychologists call "lines of development").

However, and this is the key point, in my 20+ years I've <u>never</u> ever, not even once, seen a person's EQ improve by lecturing them about what it is.

Stop talking about emotional intelligence. You are wasting your breath and the listener's time, attention and energy.

This is a somewhat nuanced but extremely important point I am making here.

This lies at the heart of what is wrong with the leadership development industry.

> *Talking about intelligence does nothing to increase it. This is akin to taking piano lessons and the instructor talks about the qualities of great piano players. The instructor goes on and on of the benefit of "musical intelligence."*

It is so obvious when we talk about other technical and complex skills (playing a musical instrument, learning to play a sport like baseball or basketball, or learning karate).

But when we talk about the technical and complex skill of leadership, people somehow miss the obvious fact that we are talking about a technical and complex skill made up of techniques and skills.

> *If you went to basketball camp, the instructors would not talk about "athletic intelligence" (kinesthetic intelligence). Rather, you would practice dribbling, passing, shooting and rebounding!*

The only time you should be talking about intelligences or "leadership traits" is when you are creating a profile for hiring. If you are in a hiring role, then yes, you want to screen and hire people with high EQ.

This book is about leadership development.

Emotional intelligence improves when and only when you give a person a specific technique, a practice, to adopt and use daily over many months.

This is the <u>only</u> way to improve these skills: through practice.

Most leadership training and coaching programs talk about "EQ" (and trust and culture and inclusivity and so on) as vague concepts and very few offer specific techniques as daily practices that actually grow these capacities.

This is the key distinction you must grasp to appreciate this groundbreaking leadership development approach.

If your objective is to improve your leadership skills rapidly, then you will want to put most of the emphasis on the specific skill sets you need to enhance the abilities you are targeting. We must come down out of the clouds of vague concepts into specific behaviors that can be memorized, practiced and matured with time (and with which we can layer on additional skills that comprise the complex abilities we associate with leadership). I previously introduced three responsibilities that have always been and always will be inherent to leadership. I call these the three *Inherent Responsibilities of Leadership*.

While these three inherent responsibilities go by many names, I have been using the common terms of *planning, teaming* and *executing*

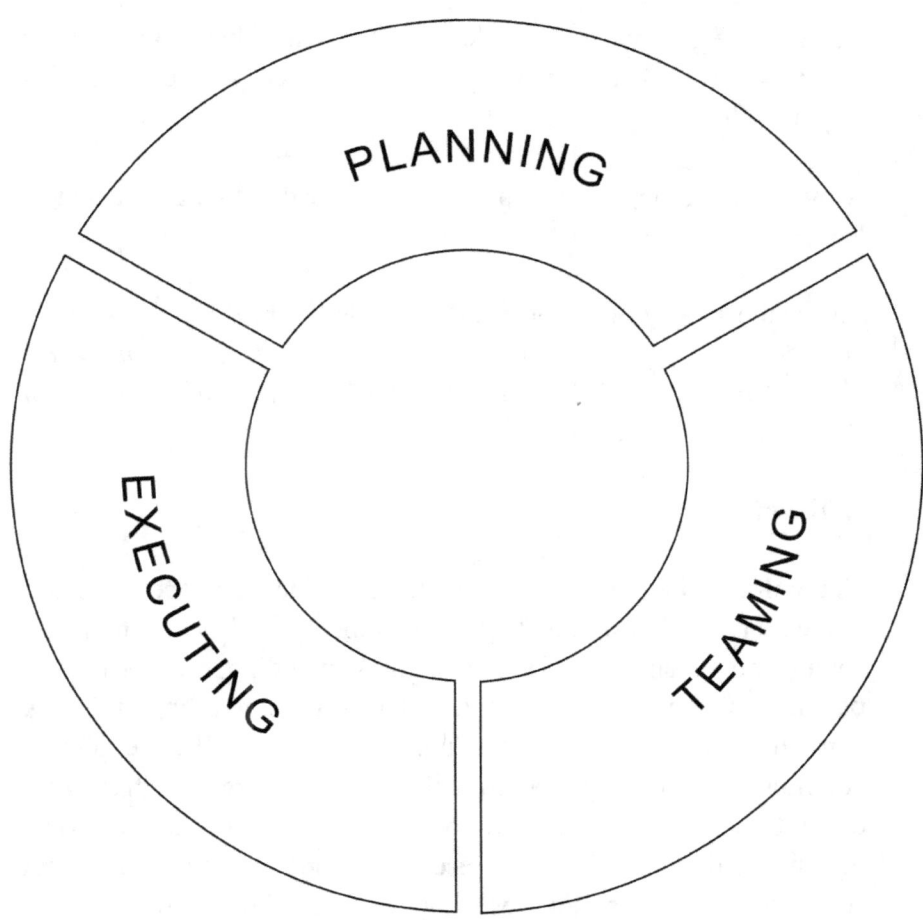

I will now begin the pivot from conventional, common ways of describing these "activities" to our more nuanced names and descriptions.

1. Planning

You will recall that leaders articulate a vision (a direction) and suggest some kind of plan to achieve that vision. They also have to align stakeholders with values and purpose of the organization and cultivate their commitment to that vision or direction, and they must guide or "steer" the organization toward that vision over time. For simplicity's sake and to feel familiar to the widest population of book readers, I've gone with the single word "planning" here, but the word "steering" would be another one-word way to describe this responsibility.

A more comprehensive and accurate title for this first dimension of leadership responsibility would be *"Strategy & Alignment."*

This is the subject of my other book entitled: *Strategy & Alignment: How the Most Successful Leaders Analyze Organizational Needs, Create Compelling Vision, Enroll and Align Stakeholders and Craft Smart, Evolving Strategic Plans.*

2. Teaming

You will recall that leaders "create the container" and "set the tone" of the relationships among the team members. The leader establishes some kind of structure for the team(s) including the norms that people are expected to follow in terms of supporting, relating, communicating and motivating. This may be explicitly communicated or simply be implicit (setting the example that others can follow). Think of this group of activities as the interpersonal dimension of leadership. I've used the word "teaming" here, but some readers may be more resonant with the word "relating."

A more comprehensive and accurate title for this second dimension of leadership responsibility would be *"Teamwork & Culture."*

This is the subject of my other book entitled: *Teamwork & Culture: How the Most Successful Leaders Set People Up for Success, Cultivate High Performance Teamwork and Leverage Communication Versatility to Keep Everyone Engaged and Motivated.*

3. Executing

As we saw earlier, this area of leadership responsibility includes guiding productive work to execute the strategy (implement the plans), managing people's performance and the projects they are working on. It is concerned with all of the activities an organization engages in, that have to do managing projects using the appropriate tools to coordinate work across teams, meeting expectations and being able to hold each other accountable to tasks, milestones, and deadlines, and making sure that people are focused on the right things and staying productive, efficient and effective. Some people think of this as "operational leadership". You may have heard the term "boots on the ground." You might also think of this dimension as the "hands" and "feet" of leadership.

A more comprehensive and accurate title for this third dimension of leadership responsibility would be *"Execution & Performance."*

As you are aware, this is the subject of this book you are currently reading

In the next section, I will pass across these three again, this time making them more comprehensive and accurate, as leadership literature would describe them, and offer a more detailed description of many of the "activities" that leaders engage in order to fulfill these responsibilities. This convention of "activities" will become extremely important.

As mentioned before, stories of great leaders and descriptions of leaders' personality traits do little (if anything) to help you become a better leader. But if you understand the activities that effective leaders do, and you learn the specific techniques (behaviors) they leverage to complete those activities successfully, then you can rapidly improve your leadership ability.

Clearly there are a lot of leadership activities that fall into these three groupings. These three abilities are comprised of skill sets, and the skill sets are, in turn, comprised of about half a dozen discrete skills (methods or techniques that have been internalized to the point that they are instinctual).

If you survey the literature on leadership, you would find dozens of discrete techniques, tactics or skills related to each of these three fundamental categories.

While there is an infinite number of techniques, methods and skills for each of these skill sets, we have found, applying Pareto's law, that it boils down to only about half a dozen specific leadership techniques / skills that matter most (for each of the nine skill sets).

This process is related to "Complex Skill Instructional Design" we discussed in the introduction chapter. This is how we learn to play baseball (throwing, catching, batting, running) or to play a musical instrument (playing notes, combining notes into chords, musical theory of keys and chord progressions, and combining these elements into songs).

> *To repeat, it is impossible to learn a complex skill (sports, martial arts, playing an instrument, flying an airplane or leadership) without breaking the complex skill down into its component parts, and then learning the technique that support each of those skills.*

Think of it this way. You and every leader you have ever worked with (or for) has drawn on these skill sets (by whatever name) to fulfill their leadership responsibilities. You may be wondering about level of skill, or level of competency. You are right to recognize that natural talent in each of these skill set areas is not evenly distributed across the population.

While all leaders engage in some version of these activities which are inherent to leadership, some are very skillful and others have not had the benefit of training and mentorship, and who may not have strong natural instincts in that area.

For example, every leader "motivates" their followers in one way or another without exception.

Similarly, even if a leader does not have any natural ability or formal training in "planning," they still make plans in some way, even if those plans are very rudimentary. Even an unsophisticated leader would say, "This is my plan."

A final example is communication. Without exception, all leaders draw upon whatever communication skills they have to coordinate efforts.

It bears repeating that these three inherent leadership responsibilities and nine skill sets are universal. Talent, training and competency level are not universal.

Some of the leaders you worked with (and for) may have been terrible at setting clear expectations, managing timelines effectively, or motivating their teams and so on, But if they were in a leadership role for long, they were in fact doing some version of the activities that fall into that "bucket" we call "performance management" "project implementation," "improving productivity."

In my other books, I define exactly what competency looks like at lower, intermediate, and higher levels of proficiency for each of the three essential abilities and all nine core competencies. While this book on *Execution & Performance* details out the benchmarks in this dimension, if you want to see the benchmarks for the other two dimensions of leadership, you can find them in my other books titled *Strategy & Alignment* and *Teamwork & Culture* (or see the conclusion section of this book for reference of my other books).

But let's not get ahead of ourselves. For now, it is helpful to just recognize the fact that these nine skill sets are fundamental to leadership and, in turn, organizational life.

You are already doing these nine things. All leaders (who are competent enough to stay in a leadership role for very long) do some versions of these nine activities in order to fulfill their responsibilities.

To provide more nuance, rather than limit ourselves to the common and familiar way of naming and thinking about each of these nine fundamental leadership skill sets, in the next section, we will introduce new terms and descriptions.

Now, continuing with our review of the essential abilities and core competencies, we will expand beyond the familiar or common labels and introduce our own terms.

For example, "Performance" becomes "Performance Management." "Alignment" becomes "Stakeholder Alignment." "Implementation" becomes "Project Implementation." And "planning" becomes "Dynamic Steering."

We are now going through another pass across the three essential abilities which represent the three buckets of activities, and the three skill sets (core competencies of leadership) under each.

We begin with the dimension I have been referring to simply as "Planning."

Strategy & Alignment

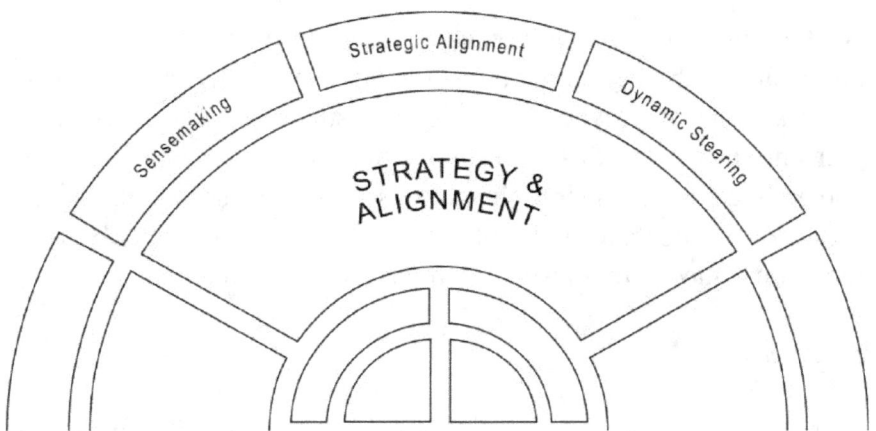

In our first pass, I called this area of responsibility simply "Planning." I will now introduce the more nuanced term, *Strategy & Alignment*.

You will recall that I defined this area of responsibility as: *establishing vision and goals, crafting strategy and plans, and enrolling stakeholder commitment.*

Strategy & Alignment includes all of the activities related to: establishing and communicating the purpose, vision, and values of the organization, making sense of what is happening in the current environment including evaluating relevant challenges and opportunities, strategic thinking, prioritizing strategic objectives, crafting strategic plans, and enrolling stakeholder commitment in the organizational vision and the strategy to achieve shared goals.

As mentioned previously, because these skill sets are fundamental and universal, you should be able to recognize the activities in each "bucket" because they are activities that you and every other leader does in one way or another (perhaps by a different name). As we unpack each skill set in later chapters, we will weave in leadership best practices which are the behaviors that skillful leaders engage when drawing upon this skill set to fulfill their leadership responsibilities.

As the saying goes, "repetition is the mother of skill." I am sure you are aware of the benefit of revisiting and reviewing key concepts, especially, as we layer in additional distinctions. I will use this convention often in this book by re-introducing previous concepts and adding another layer of nuance. As we make a second pass over these core competencies, I will replace the simple, commonly used terms introduced previously with my more nuanced terms.

Sensemaking

This skill set is concerned with your ability to evaluate the landscape (both external conditions as well as internal organizational dynamics) to determine what is really happening, the key drivers impacting the environment, what is most important for your organization, and what is most needed.

Stakeholder Alignment

This skill set is concerned with your ability to establish and articulate your organization's direction in the form of vision, values and purpose, then to align all key stakeholders so that they feel and demonstrate a shared commitment to it.

Dynamic Steering

This skill set is concerned with your ability to develop and evolve organizational strategies, establish and revise goals and objectives, and prioritize the highest-leverage projects that will lead to desired outcomes each quarter and each year.

Teamwork & Culture

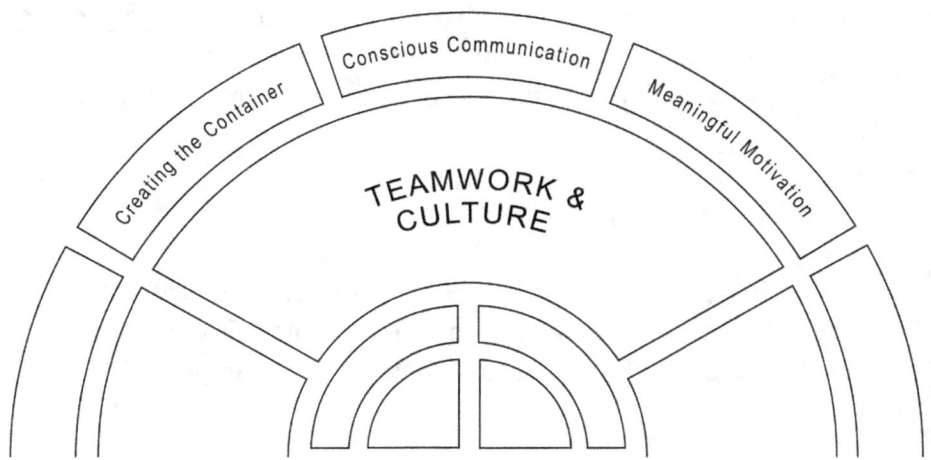

In our first pass, I called this area of responsibility and this "essential ability" simply "Teaming." I will now introduce a more nuanced term, "Teamwork & Culture."

I define this area of responsibility as: *Setting your team(s) up for success with the appropriate structure and culture, and supporting and communicating with them to keep them optimally engaged and motivated.*

Teamwork & Culture includes all of the activities related to setting your people up for success, creating and maintaining a conducive environment including a healthy culture and emotional climate, keeping people engaged and motivated using appropriate and effective communication, including feedback, listening, collaboration, and managing conflict.

Next, I will very briefly introduce each of the three skill sets that leaders draw upon to fulfill their responsibilities associated with this dimension. And I will replace the commonly-used terms, with more nuanced names.

Creating the Container

This skill set is concerned with your ability to set people up for success— this includes equipping teams with the structure, culture, training, tools and support they need to achieve shared organizational goals.

Conscious Communication

This skill set is concerned with effective communication which involves social awareness, listening, framing, feedback, dialog, collaboration, working with assumptions and interpretations, and managing conflict.

Meaningful Motivation

This skill set is concerned with keeping people engaged and motivated by understanding their needs, values, and intrinsic motivators, and appealing to each person's particular worldview and leadership preferences.

Execution & Performance

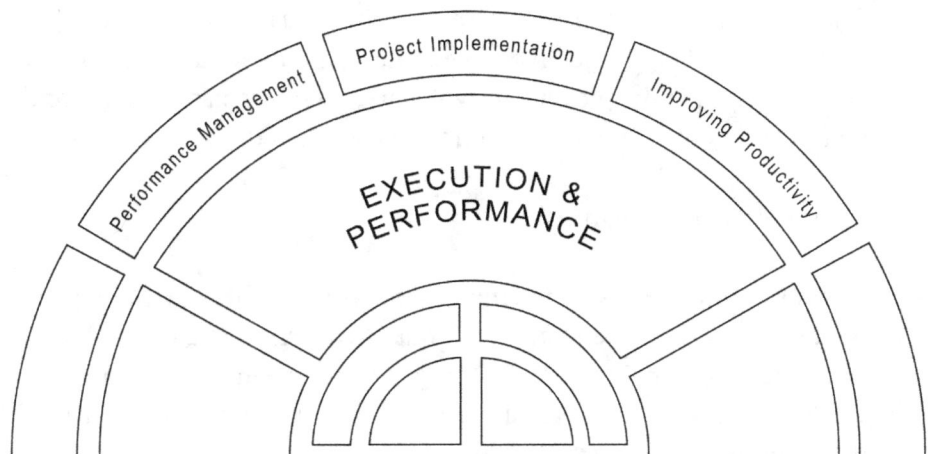

In our first pass, I called this area of responsibility and this "essential ability" simply "Executing." I will now introduce a more nuanced term, *"Execution & Performance."*

For review, I defined this area of responsibility as: *guiding productive work to execute the strategy, coordinating work, implementing projects, and managing people's performance.*

Execution & Performance, includes all of the activities related to establishing roles and responsibilities, identifying and closing performance gaps, planning and managing projects using the appropriate tools to coordinate work across teams, and maintaining high productivity so that the organizational resources are used efficiently to achieve shared goals in the desired time frames.

Performance Management

This skill set involves managing performance so that responsibilities, expectations, and agreements are consistently met, including ongoing "accountability conversations" to manage commitments and breakdowns when expectations are not met.

Project Implementation

This skill set is concerned with planning quarterly and monthly projects, defining objectives, workstreams, tasks and timelines, coordinating the people and activities necessary to stay on track and consistently complete projects on time and on budget.

Improving Productivity

The last skill set is concerned with your ability to help your organization complete work in a productive, organized, efficient and effective way, including managing calendars and tasks, running effective meetings, and staying focused and proactive in the face of distractions, urgencies and obstacles.

Now that we have established a high-level understanding of the nine skill sets that leaders draw upon (at whatever level of ability they currently possess) to fulfill their responsibilities, we can take bold steps toward our goal of rapidly increasing your leadership competency.

To draw again on our previously-used baseball analogy, soon we will enter the "batting cage" to work on our ability to hit the ball. But we have one more important foundation to lay that is necessary for success with an accelerating learning effort. But first, will take a close look at the four universal "follower mindsets" that unequivocally dictate which style of leadership a person will find credible, resonant and will want to follow.

Using the Right Style with the Right Followers

A person's worldview dictates how they see the world, what they believe is true about the world and the people in it, and what they value.

For leaders to be viewed as credible, they must match the correct leadership style with the followers' worldview. This is the key to all "resonant" leadership.

When a leader uses a leadership style that is associated with a worldview different from the follower's, this signals to the follower that this leader "doesn't get it." Put another way, the follower sees the leader as out of touch, clueless, not understanding what is really important, or not getting how the world really works.

A lack of "worldview alignment" results in the follower seeing the leader as not credible, not competent, or in the worst case, not trustworthy.

This is the key to what Ken Wilber and our academic colleagues call "integral leadership" which is another word for integrally-informed leadership, that is, leadership that is informed by integral psychology.

This is one of the main things that sets this leadership development approach apart from most of the other leadership learning methods available in the market.

Our approach to leadership is informed by a nuanced understanding of psychology, in particular, integral psychology which incorporates developmental psychology, worldviews and value systems, all of which are essential for effective leadership.

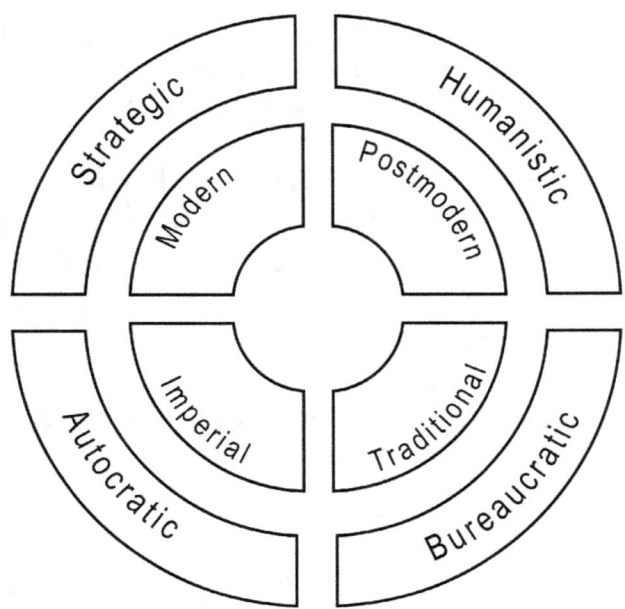

You will recall this diagram from the Universal Leadership Model that shows the four leadership styles lined up with the follower worldviews. This is absolutely essential.

As I have explained, if you use the wrong leadership style with the wrong person you run the risk of destroying your leadership credibility with that person; you will very likely appear clueless and possibly even foolish.

After teaching this unique approach to leadership to thousands of executives in corporate America, I can tell you with experience and authority that this leadership practice of "aligning leadership style with "follower mindsets" has the power to unlock and amplify the potency of the other principles and practices associated with leadership.

Using the correct "leadership style" that matches the follower's (or team's) worldview amplifies the effectiveness of every other technique described in this book and my other on leadership.

"Leadership sensemaking" is most fundamentally about "perspective taking." An integral approach to leadership involves using numerous frameworks as "lenses" which provide visibility into dimensions of reality that conventional leaders are unaware of, overlook, or ignore. The result of these superior (more accurate) lenses and precision perspective-taking practices is greater awareness, better approaches, and more skillful action.

While "matching styles with mindsets" is central to this revolutionary method, it does not represent the totality of it. Rather, it provides a logical and helpful orienting framework—like the conventions of North, South, East, West on a geographical map—to ensure that the leader is headed in the right direction. As you read this section, please be mindful of the fact that this is merely an introduction, a high-level overview of this framework. The goal is for you to become familiar with it. The application of these leadership styles (to all of the different abilities and skill sets) will come with time. It should be obvious that understanding the mindset of your followers (or your team or culture) is central to leadership effectiveness. In fact, most comprehensive leader development programs teach some methods for "understanding people."

Some simply teach listening skills, many teach various kinds of personality typology systems, and a few use stages of development (a.k.a. stages of psychological maturity) to help leaders better understand their followers and what makes them tick.

I'm going to use an American idiom—being "in the ballpark"—as an analogy to illustrate a crucial point. Those personality types, situational leadership tactics, and get-to-know-your-people methods are like finding your section and seat at a large baseball game.

Assuming that you are in the correct stadium, knowing the exact section, row and seat number is very helpful. But here's the catch. In this analogy, your followers' worldview (their values and universal beliefs) represents the stadium. If you fail to accurately recognize your followers' worldview, then you are not even in the right ballpark; therefore, the details about personality types and behavioral tendencies (even a person's goals) are essentially useless.

Worldview is the overall perspective from which one sees and interprets the world.

> *A person's worldview defines what they care about, what motivates them, what they believe is worthwhile, and what they believe lacks value or is "wrong." And as we now understand it also specifically dictates which leadership style they will be resonant with, and follow, as well as which approaches are likely to backfire.*

If you want to understand people, you first need to get "into the right ballpark" by identifying their worldview.

I believe that the failure to grasp meaning making systems—what I am calling worldviews here—lies at the heart of the problem with conventional approaches to leadership. Those approaches often wrongly assume that people's motivations are homogenous. Most conventional approaches to leadership (and also management) fail to adequately take into account the fact that people with different worldviews value different things, interpret the same facts differently, and subsequently have very different priorities. This mistake is at the heart of the "bogus leadership advice" most so-called experts offer.

Follower Mindsets Are the Key to Leadership Success

I mentioned Barbara Kellerman (author of *Bad Leadership, The End of Leadership* and *Professionalizing Leadership*) and Jeffrey Pfeffer (author of *Leadership BS)* in the introduction. Unfortunately, these two courageous "whistleblowers" are among only a few leadership experts that are acknowledging the fact that most leadership development programs focus mainly on the leader and generally ignore "context" in which the leadership is occurring. Worse, they almost all leave the followers out of the equation altogether.

Yes, you read that right. The majority of leadership training programs mostly or completely ignore the followers!

They focus the vast majority of the time talking about traits of great leaders and qualities of effective leaders with seemingly no awareness at all of the needs, worldviews and preferences of the followers. This, again, is one of the main reasons that most leadership development programs produce such criminally dismal results. In her books, Kellerman really takes the leadership industry to talk over this colossal error. She underscores the fact that any legitimate approach to leadership must take into account all three elements of the leader, the context (the circumstances), and especially the followers.

I would suggest that one of the most important aspects of a leader's context or circumstances, is their follower's worldviews. If you understand the follower's worldview (or mindset, then you will know what they care about, what is important to them, how they define leadership, and what they look for in a person they view as a credible leader.

Most importantly, if you know a person's "follower mindset," and you know how to match up the mindsets with the four Universal Leadership Styles, then you can avoid the embarrassing situation of using the wrong style with the wrong person and destroying your leadership credibility in their eyes.

In the same way that beauty is in the eye of the beholder, leadership is in the eye of the follower. If you use the wrong leadership style with the wrong person they will not see you as a credible leader. They will see you as clueless or even foolish. A leadership approach that is extremely resonant with one employee, team or department will be ineffective or even offensive for another. The troublesome issue is:

"How can you know which approach will be effective and which will be offensive?"

The answer, of course, is the follower's worldview.

As I mentioned in the section about the Leadership Rosetta Stone, integral psychology shows us that about 95% of the values/belief systems that today's leaders are likely to encounter fall into four broad worldviews.

For some readers, this fact is not new. Many readers are already familiar with Modern, Postmodern, and Traditional worldviews. However, few people are aware of the fact that these "value systems" predict with astonishing accuracy which leadership style will be resonant and appreciated, and which styles will be met with resistance and/or rejection.

It is hard to overstate the significance of this. This realization lies at the heart of the breakthrough that my team discovered, with Ken Wilber's guidance in the early 2000s. Essentially, this deceptively simple Universal Leadership Model successfully aggregates, synthesizes, and integrates, more than a 100 years of leadership theories.

Moreover, once sufficiently internalized in practice (and that takes a little time of course), this unique leadership framework allows leaders to effectively motivate and influence followers (of all kinds) with a level of precision and efficacy that is rarely witnessed.
Also, this works everywhere it has been tested. In corporate environments, financial services, construction sites, assembly lines, hospitals, police forces, military... even in remote African tribal villages.

Values Research

Worldviews are composed of values and universal beliefs. Values are perceptual filters minds use to determine ("evaluate") what is important in any given situation. Universal beliefs are broad-based beliefs about self, others, and system (how the world is perceived to work). In terms of knowing which leader a given person is likely to follow (or elect given the choice), in terms of knowing what people care about, in terms of knowing what motivates people, in terms of understanding people in the most fundamental sense, nothing is more germane than values.

The conceptualization and use of values models is widespread and informed by a multitude of different approaches that differ in details but are quite similar in principle and overarching conclusions. Values research is widely used by psychologists, political scientists, and marketers. The pervasive role of values in all aspects of human life has motivated hundreds of studies in the disciplines of psychology, sociology, cultural anthropology, and consumer behavior.

A large body of research has shown conclusively that values represent both a powerful explanation of and influence on a variety of individual and collective behaviors. In fact, in recent years, the study and measurement of values has become one of the most dynamic research areas in the social science disciplines (management, leadership, marketing and consumer behavior). Several values measurement methodologies are currently available and more are surfacing.

These worldviews, along with their correlating universal leadership styles, cut across nationalities, ethnicity, and culture. There is nothing inherently American or North American (or European or Caucasian) about these worldviews and leadership styles. However, I live in the U.S. and most of my work has involved leaders in the Americas. The examples and illustrations in my teaching reflect my experience.

Also, in this presentation, I often use the term "mindset" in place of or in addition to the more academic term "worldview."

When describing people who hold a worldview, it is often helpful to use the word "mindset" in place of the word worldview. Rather than say, this person holds a modern worldview, we could say, this person has a "modern mindset" or better still, this person has an "achiever mindset." This section of the book will follow this convention and will use "mindset" in place of "worldview." This presentation uses broad and simplified examples of single worldviews or mindsets that help new students become familiar with their basic appearance and function. Once you can begin to recognize them, in time you will begin to see how they can be combined (as some people's mindset is a blend of two such as 50/50 or 60/40).

Next, I will go through each of the four follower mindsets, describe how the world looks through that lens, refer to the massive amount of research that backs up these assertions, and give you several examples of "profiles" of employees who typify this mindset. After the explanation of the follower mindset, then I will offer a more detailed explanation of the style of leadership that should be used with people with that mindset.

Achiever Mindset

People with a modern worldview can also be described as having an "Achiever mindset." They identify with being highly rational, competitive, ambitious, autonomous and elite. They emphasize success and/or status as defined by material acquisition and "upward mobility."

They value excellence, advancement, prosperity, achievement, and status. Most importantly, they prefer to follow leaders who are perceived to have the most expertise and ability to achieve goals. In other words, they follow leaders who use the Strategic Leadership style.

The Achiever mindset (and the Strategic Leadership style) is well suited for the following environments and circumstances: sales departments, professional services firms, innovation-driven organizations, senior management positions, and in roles that require advanced levels of education such as scientific research.

Seeing the World Through an Achiever's Lens

In academic circles, this worldview is referred to as the "Modern worldview" (as contrasted to the Traditional and Postmodern worldviews).

When you look at the world through this lens, you see a playing field full of possibilities to explore and opportunities to achieve. You will emphasize the scientific and rational dimensions of what you see. The key to life is to strive for, and achieve "success."

Through this lens, it becomes easy to believe in the advancement of humankind through the application of the highly disciplined rational mind and its scientific, technological, and medical manifestations. Life is to be met and mastered by finding the best way to act on its limitless opportunities.

Empirical Research

While this worldview, or "follower mindset" may be new for a few readers, there is nothing new, novel or controversial about it; in fact, my descriptions are based on widely-accepted and respected empirical research that has come out of Harvard, Yale, Boston College, Washington University and other top institutions over the last four decades. I offer more nuanced, academic analysis in other books (especially my book series on Integral Leadership). For this introduction, I will mention the academic terms that the different leading psychologists use for this worldview / follower mindset. McClelland uses the term "Achievement," Loevinger uses "Conscientious," Kohlberg uses "Social Order," Graves uses

"Multiplistic-Achievist," Kegan uses "Institutional," Wade uses "Achievement," and Torbert uses "Achiever." When I'm using "follower mindset" terminology, I say Achiever mindset and when I'm using the worldview term, I call it the Modern worldview. Although I don't use Ken Wilber's color schemes in this book series created for mainstream readers, for my readers who are students of integral theory, I will mention here that the Wilberian color code for this worldview is "orange."

Understanding People with an Achiever Mindset

People with this mindset tend to believe that while there are many valid ways to think and behave, there is always one best way. People with this mindset want to feel they are at the "top of their game" and that they have earned (quite literally, in some cases) the recognition of belonging to an elite group.

They are not satisfied to simply "play by the rules;" rather, they want to fully understand the rules to gain a competitive advantage over those with less acuity, with the ultimate ambition of becoming so successful that they might eventually "change the rules of the game." Many of their decisions will be motivated by the promise of success and status, as well as an awareness and fairly sophisticated understanding of the dynamics of the overall system within which they operate (company, church, nation, global marketplace).

Some examples of occupational roles that tend to epitomize the Achiever mindset include salespeople, attorneys, research scientists, marketing agents, PR and advertising representatives, elected public officials, architects, and physicians in conventional practice (as opposed to alternative medicine which would very likely be someone with a Pluralistic mindset described in the next section). Following are some example profiles of people with these mindsets.

Rob - Research Scientist

I'm a research scientist who's convinced that most of the world's problems can be solved with the right technological advancements and tools. I think that many people hold superstitious, irrational beliefs that are detrimental to society's interests and retard scientific progress. While I enjoy my work during the week, I pursue my real passion on the weekends. I've completed over twenty triathlons and placed in the top five in most of them. My training schedule could probably qualify as some sort of third world form of punishment, but when I cross the finish line in first place it's all worth it. There's a force in me that's relentless in its determination to win. There's something exhilarating about testing your limits and pushing your personal edge.

Danielle - Attorney

I just graduated from Harvard Law School and I am joining one of the most prestigious firms in the country. I grew up in a two-parent working class household and was a latch-key kid. My parents were focused on providing necessities for us. They helped me to see that hard work and determination are keys to success. While I respect my parents "traditional" ways, I knew from a young age that I wanted to work smarter, not harder, to enjoy the finer things in life. And while my parents' religious orientation works for them, I wasn't satisfied with simplistic answers to complex questions. To be honest, I believe that the world would be a better place if more people would put their faith in reason and look to science rather than religion for answers.

Lee - Small Business Owner

I own a small web-based company that produces and sells custom laptop cases for the fashion-conscious consumer. As a start-up, I wasn't entirely sure what I was doing but decided to take some calculated risks while telling myself that failing wasn't an option. I became incredibly focused and goal-oriented, and within two years I was featured as Entrepreneur of the Year in a nation-wide magazine.

Strategic Leadership

People like Lee, Danielle and Rob who have an Achiever worldview prefer to follow leaders who embody personal excellence and success and who are perceived to be most likely to achieve predefined goals.

In this form of leadership, the person with the most expertise leads via strategic planning and tangible incentives. It is characterized by incentivizing teams to execute well-conceived plans to outperform their competitors. In academic terms, this approach is sometimes referred to as "transactional" to differentiate it from the "transformational" quality of the Collaborative Leadership style.

It's easy to see how the Achiever mindset finds this strategic, goal-oriented leadership approach resonant.

In fact, as we shall see, the developers and advocates of the many "schools of leadership" that fall into this category nearly always possess the corresponding worldview.

This explains why academics / researchers / authors who are enthusiastic proponents of each leadership style believe that their style is the best and should be used in every situation.

When you are with a group of people who share the same values system, if you pay attention to their language, you will notice that they have a way of communicating with each other that reflects their common values and beliefs.

My mentor Ken Wilber refers to this as the "Dominant Mode of Discourse." I use the shorter term "Values Dialect" (or simply dialect). This values dialect is the dialect of business.

Leaders whose primary mindset is Affiliative or Traditional who want to be taken seriously in business need to learn to speak the Achiever dialect even if it is not their "native tongue."

Affiliative Mindset

People with an affiliative mindset identify with being nonjudgmental, egalitarian, and socially and environmentally conscious.

They value connection, tolerance, cultural sensitivity, diversity, sustainability, and interdependence. They strive for fulfillment as defined by personal growth, increased awareness, harmonious relationships, and "making a difference."

Most importantly, they prefer to follow leaders who are perceived as being aware, sensitive to the wellbeing of others, value consensus, and always treat others as equals; in other words, leaders who use a Humanistic leadership style. My colleagues and I also refer to this style as the "Collaborative" leadership style. I will use both terms in this book series.

Seeing the World Through an Affiliative Lens

In academic circles, this worldview is referred to as the "Postmodern Worldview" (as opposed to the Modern or Traditional). It is sometimes also called a "pluralistic" worldview.

Sociologist and bestselling author Paul Ray uses the term "Cultural Creatives" to describe people who identify with the worldview. In his book *The Cultural Creatives: How 50 Million People Are Changing the World*, he summarizes research on 50 million adult Americans (slightly over one quarter of the adult population). Ray presents a significant amount of demographic and psychographic research comparing and contrasting this worldview to the Traditional worldview and Modern worldview.

When you look at the world through this Postmodern or "pluralistic" lens, you see a diverse ecosystem where cooperation leads to synergy.

The dictionary definition of pluralistic is: "a social perspective that believes no single explanatory system or view of reality can account for all the phenomena of life; rather there are many (plural) truths. Further, it is desirable to have numerous distinct ethnic, religious, or cultural groups present and tolerated in society."

Empirical Research

My descriptions in this book are all based on empirical research out of Harvard, Yale, Boston College, Washington University and other top institutions over the last four decades. For this introduction, I will mention the academic terms that the different leading psychologists use for this worldview / follower mindset. McClelland uses the term "Affiliative," Loevinger uses "Individualistic," Kohlberg uses "Social Contract," Graves uses "Relativistic-Personalistic," Kegan uses "late-institutional" into "early-Interindividual," Wade uses "Affiliative," and Torbert uses "Individualist." Although I don't use Ken Wilber's color schemes in this book series created for mainstream readers, for my readers who are students of integral theory, I will mention here that the Wilberian color code for this worldview is "green."

Understanding People with an Affiliative Mindset

Historically, leaders with the postmodern worldview and Affiliative mindset were responsible for the human rights and environmental movements.

People with this mindset tend to display egalitarian, tolerant attitudes, and are often enthusiastic endorsers of equal rights and equal opportunity for all people in all situations. People with this mindset want to feel as though they are "making a difference."

Their decisions tend to be motivated by the belief that their choice will help them (or their organization) continue to grow and develop, and that the world will be positively impacted (or at least not negatively affected) by their actions.

Whereas, people with the Achiever mindset emphasize external/material accomplishments (financial success, material acquisitions, status), people with this Affiliative mindset prefer to emphasize internal/intangible accomplishments (awareness, human connection, emotional fulfillment).

As such, they are more motivated by personal growth, people, and relationships than by material gain.

Of course this group can be highly motivated to achieve material success for a social or environmental cause as long as this is accomplished without sacrifices of personal growth or rewarding relationships.

People with this mindset gravitate toward communities that value tolerance for multiple perspectives, interdependence, creativity, diversity, activism, and "progressive" approaches.

They prefer nontraditional, "humanized" workplaces where self-expression is encouraged and rewarded; where contribution to social, political, and environmental causes is mission-critical or intrinsic to profitability; where duties and roles are actively interchanged in the service of a nonhierarchical, egalitarian approach; where team and roundtable gatherings are standard to internal operations and decision-making; where the job requires higher education; and where ongoing growth and development along with "work-life-balance" are encouraged. Following, I provide some profiles of people with this Affiliative mindset. I am certain one of these profiles (if not more than one) will remind you of someone you know. Pay attention to these patterns, they are all around you, and the sooner you begin to recognize them, the sooner you will know which leadership style or approach will be resonant with them.

Jonathan - Volunteer

Right out of college I joined the Peace Corps. At some point during my senior year, I realized that most of the world's population will never have the opportunities I once took for granted. Today, I work as a diversity consultant in the public sector, I help people within organizations accept and find strength in each others' differences. There's a real tendency in all of us to feel that our own way of looking at things is intrinsically superior, and it's this attitude that is responsible for most of the world's conflict. If everyone would accept each other's differences, we'd finally have a peaceful planet.

Delia - Record Label Owner

At eighteen, I founded my own music label because I wanted to promote social justice and retain artistic integrity that a corporate mentality wouldn't allow. After selling over 50,000 of my albums, the major labels came courting with huge deals. Because they wanted me to compromise, I declined. Today, my label is an internationally known icon for independent art, political action, and grassroots sponsorship.

Larry - Physician

I'm an MD and the founder of a holistic health care company that's committed to people and the planet first and profit second. I've taken great care to give everyone in my organization an equal voice; there is no hierarchy to speak of, and decision-making is done by consensus. As far as I'm concerned, a good business should function a lot like a democracy to ensure that too much power isn't invested in any one person. It's clear to me that the modern lifestyle being commercialized and relentlessly promoted by megacorporations is environmentally unsustainable for the planet. When I recognized I was part of the problem, I decided to become part of the solution by simplifying my life and limiting my consumption.

Humanistic Leadership

People like Larry, Delia and Jonathon who have an Affiliative mindset prefer to follow leaders who are perceived as being aware, sensitive to the wellbeing of others, value consensus, and treat others as equals. People with the Affiliative mindset believe that leadership is not vested in any single person; rather, it should be consensus-based in the sense that self-managed teams should lead themselves.

This approach is considered "transformational" and involves inviting people's perceptions, feelings and intuition via roundtable discussion and dialog to arrive at consensus, then work collaboratively toward common goals that serve the greater good. It is also called "Collaborative" leadership. Leadership is also likely to be understood as situational and temporary; nearly all position-based authority is therefore highly questionable or even rejected outright. Unlike the Traditional mindset, people with the Affiliative mindset abhor hierarchy and will tend to either ignore it or seek to actively undermine it.

Many of the books that promote work-life balance, emotionally-aware "resonant" leadership, and "appreciative inquiry" are both popular with people having a Affiliative mindset and were written by people with Affiliative mindsets. Katzenbach and Smith's bestselling book, *The Wisdom of Teams,* was mentioned earlier in the leadership theory section of this book.

When authors are subject to their own worldview (and fail to recognize the different worldviews at play in the workplace), they tend to advocate their approach as the best approach. This is another example of the rampant unconscious worldview bias that we see in this field of leadership development.

In fact, it is Humanistic leadership (also called "transformational leadership" or "collaborative leadership") that is currently in the vanguard of popular business literature. For many leaders, this humanistic, transformational approach is a welcome shift away from the transactional and traditional (Authority) approaches that have been popular for so long. However, sophisticated leaders see the flaw in this thinking. There is no best leadership approach for all types of people. The best leadership approach is the one that will be most resonant with the people you hope to lead.

Humanistic leadership works great with people with Affiliative mindsets. However, people with an Achiever mindset consider it to be too touchy-feely, people with a Traditional mindset consider its relativistic values to be immoral, and people with a Power mindset interpret kindness and sensitivity as weaknesses and steamroll right over it.

Traditional Mindset

People with a Traditional Mindset identify with being responsible, purposeful, and self-sacrificing. They seek a reassuring sense of stability, security, and belonging by conforming to a worldview that they unambiguously describe as the tried and true "natural order of things."

This natural order of things is defined by the long-standing traditions of the culture in which they were socialized. As you would expect, people with this mindset prefer to follow leaders who are perceived as having positional and/or moral authority; in other words, leaders who use an Authoritarian Leadership style.

Seeing the World Through a Traditional Lens

You no doubt recognize that this is what academics refer to as the "Traditional worldview" (contrasting it with the familiar Modern and Postmodern Worldviews).

When you look through this Traditional lens, you see an ordered existence under the control of a higher authority and ultimate Truth.

Although amber is the integral theory color code we associate with this worldview, when you look through the lens, what you actually see is black-and-white.

People who use this lens to view the world perceive a concrete, literal, dualistic world of right and wrong, insiders and outsiders, believers and non-believers, and good and evil. They also see people who conform to rigid traditional roles (such as man earning money and women staying home and raising children) as following the "natural order of things" and people who deviate from conventional roles (such as people who are gender fluid, non-binary or identify as trans) as aberration at best and evil at worst.

If you know what to look for it is very easy to spot people with this Traditional mindset.

Empirical Research

My descriptions are all based on empirical research from Harvard, Yale, Boston College, Washington University and other top institutions over the last four decades. For this introduction, I will mention the academic terms that the different leading psychologists use for this worldview / follower mindset. McClelland uses the term "Authority," Loevinger uses "Conformist," Kohlberg uses "Interpersonal Accord" and "Conformity," Graves uses "Absolutistic-Obedience," Kegan uses "Interpersonal," Wade uses "Conformist," and Torbert uses "Diplomat."

When I'm using "follower mindset" terminology, I say Traditional mindset and Traditional worldview. Although I don't use Ken Wilber's color schemes in this book series created for mainstream readers, for my readers who are students of integral theory, I will mention here that the Wilberian color code for this worldview is "amber." Also some readers may be familiar with the National Values Center / Spiral Dynamics colors, which is "blue" for this mindset.

Understanding People with a Traditional Mindset

People with Traditional mindsets tend to be dedicated, reliable, loyal, responsible, conscientious, and can be expected to think and act in routine, predictable ways.

They are oriented around learning and following the rules defined by authority, and are more than willing to subjugate their own impulses and desires in the service of a greater calling, cause, or mission that they find meaningful, purposeful and in accord with their traditional beliefs.

While "Blue Collar jobs" are typical, people with this mindset are especially attracted to work that promotes what they consider to be the moral good (e.g., ministers, teachers, police officers, guidance counselors, children's athletic coaches, etc.). In addition to preferring jobs that require routine and discipline, this group thrives in circumstances that others might view as repetitive or tedious. Consequently, they excel in standards and compliance roles as well as organizational and system maintenance jobs.

People with this Traditional mindset value hierarchy; therefore, they respond best to clearly defined rules, deadlines, responsibilities and a well-defined chain of command. They also appreciate a written code of conduct to refer to, especially one that offers clear protocols for action and predictable consequences for success and failure.

Wherever in the world you encounter the Traditional worldview, it will define acceptable and unacceptable gender roles, sexual orientations and practices, food and drink consumption, and of course spiritual practices based on the long-standing traditions endemic to the culture they were raised in.

For people with this Traditional mindset, there is one and only one right way to think and behave. Conforming to authority's prescribed "right" way to think and behave is the key to ensure future rewards.

It is very important to understand that while the details of the local customs and culture (including religious practices) will differ, the broad-based core values and universal beliefs that comprise a Traditional worldview will be identical anywhere on the planet, whether it be Tehran, Turkey, Thailand or West Texas.

As an integrally-informed leader, you must understand that in Traditional cultures, both Modern and Postmodern values tend to be viewed not only with skepticism and suspicion, but often with fear and in some cases, hatred.

Fear is a major motivator underlying a feeling of "us vs. them" in the form of a common enemy that threatens the traditional way of life of the traditional lifestyle.

Proponents of the Traditional worldview (regardless of country or culture) understand these drives inherently and use positional or perceived moral authority to galvanize loyalty and motivate followers (or perhaps to gain views and viewers or sell books).

In the U.S., books such as Sean Hannity's *Deliver Us from Evil* and Bill O'Reilly's *Culture Warrior* make a convincing case that Modern and Postmodern values are a dangerous threat to the traditional way of life. So do Ann Coulter's books and Tucker Carlson's talk show episodes. These are all good examples of this fear and hatred of worldviews that deviate from the traditional view and traditional lifestyle.

The traditional mindset is based on a "parental orientation" to reality that is binary, there are parents and children and not much in between.

The leader is a parental figure and the followers are like children who should obey. The leader is seen as the authority. This is why in leadership theory, it is referred to as "authoritarian" leadership. For the traditional mindset, the authority (who is in the position of parent) should tell the followers (who are in the position of children) how to work, succeed, be moral, and generally live a good life (according to God's plan or according to the "one true way").

> *To an individual who holds this Traditional worldview, the person that has been annointed, appointed or elected is the de facto leader.*

People with a traditional mindset view leadership as "positional." So the "Minister" and the "Mayor" are the defacto leaders.

There is one very important exception to this principle.

If the appointed or elected person does <u>not</u> share their traditional values and beliefs, then they will be rejected. This is very important to understand.

In this scenario, the elected leader is viewed as *illegitimate, a fake, a fraud,* or an *opportunist* who is only doing it for egocentric gain, and should be removed from that position as quickly as possible, in some cases, by any means necessary!

This reliably explains and predicts the right-wing behavior toward elected leaders viewed as "liberals."

Perhaps there is no better example of this than how the United States traditional values voters reacted to the election of Barack Obama. They (with rare exceptions) despised him, because they fear and often hate leaders that do not share their traditional values and beliefs. We saw this again when Joe Biden was elected as U.S. president.

Note that I said "that they believe" follow their traditional values. Unfortunately it is not difficult for actual opportunists (a.k.a. "autocrats") who do not actually have traditional beliefs to convince gullible traditional voters that they do share their traditional beliefs in order to win their support or their votes.

This is why it is very common for traditional voters to vote against their own best interests and to elect politicians who are actually just manipulating them.

Following, I will share some profiles of stereotypical traditional mindset followers. I'm sure you will recognize one or all three of these profiles as employees, colleagues, or perhaps members of your family. Try to look for those patterns.

Once you learn to recognize these mindsets in others, you will know exactly which of the four universal leadership styles they will find resonant, will trust and will willingly follow and for whom they will offer their discretionary effort.

Recall earlier, I said that if you use the wrong leadership style with the wrong follower, they will not see you as credible, worse, they may see you as clueless or even foolish.

Here is a real-life example of that principle in action.

If you use a Humanistic leadership style (a.k.a. collaborative, transformational or "self-managed teams") with one of these people, it will destroy your credibility in their eyes. They will see you as just "not getting it" (that is you don't get how the world really is). And they may see you as clueless, or even foolish.

So as you read about John, Susan and Daniel on the following pages, use this opportunity to find your followers in these descriptions!

John - True Believer

It's true, I've been called "straight laced" more than once. But people who know the Truth have a duty to defend it, even if it means being politically incorrect. People talk about "shades of gray" but as far as I'm concerned, right is right and wrong is wrong. Ultimately, almost everything is black and white, and those who suggest otherwise are just avoiding moral responsibility.

Susan - School Counselor

I love God, my family, and my country—in that order. I'm particularly proud of my nationality—when I hear people criticizing the leaders of my country I tend to feel rather insulted and often angry. I really feel that some things are simply not ours to question, and that obedience and loyalty are the highest virtues to which a person can aspire for. I work as a school counselor. I'm sometimes baffled why so many of today's kids go to such great lengths to be "different." By striving to be such "non-conformists" they don't fit in. Also, I feel frustrated by our school's tolerance for modes of dress and conduct that I find socially unacceptable and are against the family values that all schools should reinforce.

Daniel - Faith-Based Counselor

I teach a vocational rehab class for single parents and one of the things I stress to my students is that if you follow the rules—both in my class and life in general—you're bound to come out all right. With the world as unpredictable as it is, it just doesn't pay to take many risks or deviate from what's been proven to work. What is most important is having stability and knowing that you and those you love will have a secure future.

Authority Leadership

People like John, Susan and Daniel who have a Traditional worldview prefer to follow leaders they perceive as having positional or moral authority, who share their traditional beliefs, and who lead using strict adherence to a "chain of command" or the "rules" of the institution that has bestowed that authority. In other words, people with traditional mindsets see the "Bureacratic" leader (also called "Authoritarian" leader) as the most credible, legitimate and trustworthy leaders.

This term, "authoritarian leadership," is, in fact, the well-researched, widely- acknowledged and accurate academic term for this authority-centric style of leadership.

For corporate audiences, especially ones that are composed of a lot of traditionalists, the term "Authority leadership" is preferred. I will use both terms in this book.

In this leadership style, the person with *positional authority* leads via chain of command. This approach is "Hierarchical" and is characterized by compliance with the rules to meet the requirements dictated by the person with authority.

While fear and guilt are primary motivators for people with a Traditional mindset, they do not want their leaders to show either of these emotions. Effective "Authority" leaders intuit this and rarely, if ever, admit they don't know something or admit when they have made a mistake, or admit they are afraid.

That kind of "vulnerability based self-disclosure works will Humanistic leadership with followers with an Affiliative mindset, but authority leaders (with Traditional followers) rarely if ever admit their mistakes, their lack of knowledge or their fears, doubts or uncertainties.

George W. Bush, a well-known authoritarian leader, understood this implicitly as he is having a "Traditional" mindset and his native style is "Authority." In his eight years as President of the United States, even in the face of incontrovertible evidence of poor judgment and costly errors (financial, military, international affairs, many millions of unnecessary deaths and so on), he never admitted making mistakes.

While many have criticized this behavior, to his credit, this was exactly what his large base of "traditional values voters" wanted to see in their leader.

People with other mindsets tend to view this trait as an inability to admit mistakes or learn from them, yet people with this Traditional mindset will describe this same behavior as "principled."

Using the same Traditional lens, popular leadership authors and theorists (including many "leadership experts") write books about the innate "character traits of leaders," the enduring "laws of leadership," or the "steps to being a great leader."

Author John Maxwell's bestselling books are excellent examples of the traditional view of leadership.

While Modern and Postmodern writers criticize what they consider to be reductionist approaches to life and leadership, it is very important to remember that advocates of this worldview (such Tucker Carlson, Glenn Beck, Sean Hannity, Ann Coulter) are so popular precisely because a large percentage of the population (estimated 40% in the U.S.) have adopted this Traditional worldview.

Integrally-informed leadership is concerned with seeing the world as it actually is and meeting people in it as they actually are. Integrally-informed leaders realize that although the Authority leadership style may lack a certain nuance as compared to other styles, it is exactly the approach that a very large percentage of the population is most resonant with.

Power Mindset

Previously, I used the word "Imperial" to describe this worldview. As mentioned previously, worldviews are a psychological and somewhat academic term. For corporate audiences, we often pivot to "mindset" terminologies to offer a more user-friendly vernacular.

Here, when describing people who hold this worldview, I will introduce a new term, the "Power-Centric Mindset" or "Power Mindset" for short.

People with a Power mindset identify with being strong, courageous risk takers, who are capable of defending themselves in a dangerous world and getting what they want, when they want it.

They emphasize personal power as defined by the ability to live outside conventional rules and gratify their desires. They value power, protection, freedom, respect, and control. Most importantly, they prefer to follow leaders who are perceived as being the strongest, toughest, and most dominant; in other words, leaders who use an Autocratic Leadership style.

Seeing the World Through a Power-Centric Lens

Academics refer to this worldview as the "Imperial worldview". It's easy to see this worldview dominating many periods of human history. You have probably heard it described as "Machiavellian."

This term derives from the book The Prince written in 1513 by Niccolo Machiavelli as a pragmatic guide to getting and keeping power in a dangerous world. In The Prince, Machiavelli famously advocates "the ends justify the means." This pretty much sums up the Imperial worldview and the Autocratic Leadership style that is best paired with it.

When you look at the world through this Power-centric lens, you see a jungle filled with predators and selfcentered people, where only the strongest and most cunning survive and thrive.

If this is your world, or at least your worldview, you tend to view others as competitors for scarce resources and will tend to interpret hesitation, softness, or even kindness, as signs of weakness.

From this point of view, team members are useful allies in the ongoing quest for power and when a common enemy is identified, the team can marshal its resources quite effectively.

To this worldview, "might" really does make "right."

The "haves" deserve their status and privilege because they are powerful and dominant, and the "have not's" deserve their status because of their weakness or incompetence. Above all, people with the Power mindset value power and respect, and will respond favorably only to leaders who are perceived to be powerful and who "command respect."

Empirical Research

My descriptions in this book are all based on empirical research out of Harvard, Yale, Boston College, Washington University and other top institutions. For this introduction, I will mention the academic terms that the different leading psychologists use for this worldview / follower mindset. McClelland uses the term "Power," Loevinger uses "Self-Protective," Kohlberg uses "Self-Interest," Graves uses "Egocentric-Exploitive," Kegan uses "Imperial," Wade uses "Egocentric," and Torbert uses "Opportunist."

When I'm using "follower mindset" terminology, I say Power mindset and when I'm using the worldview term, I call it the Imperial worldview. Although I don't use Ken Wilber's color schemes in this book series created for mainstream readers, for my readers who are students of integral theory, I will mention here that the Wilberian color code for this worldview is "red."

Understanding People with a Power Mindset

People who identify with the Power mindset tend to be persuasive, egocentric, courageous, impulsive, and often charismatic. People with this mindset play crucial roles in society: the need for people who possess great courage and inner strength, and are willing to take enormous risks. However, people with this mindset are not always appreciated, because they also tend to be fiercely independent—"I live by my rules alone" and are disinterested in conforming to the status quo (including many societal norms). They have a tendency to think mainly of themselves and can be insensitive to others' needs and desires in their own uncompromising push to break free from limits, satisfy their desires, or impose their will.

Although both the Power and Achiever mindsets are driven to "win" or "dominate", the "Achiever" drive is fueled by excellence / competitiveness / status while the Power mindset is motivated by power / respect / glory. The Imperial worldview and this Power mindset can be found in every socioeconomic system, but may be more readily noticeable in inner cities and in isolated rural areas.

It is common to encounter people with this mindset in tough environments such as reform schools, heavy construction, oil and gas refineries, and prisons. These are the life conditions that give rise to and reward Power mindsets. Oftentimes people with a Power mindset were raised in or spent many years in these life conditions. When they move on to new circumstances they may carry that worldview with them. As you would expect, people with this mindset gravitate toward social groups that value toughness, aggression, and physical prowess and that encourage behavior sometimes considered "beneath social norms."

Following are profiles of people with a Power mindset. As with the other profiles I have provided in this book, please use these as archetypes and think about how these profiles remind you of some of the people in your life, or perhaps former bosses or co-workers.

People with this Power mindset do not respond well to "Strategic" leadership, to " Humanistic" (or "Inclusive") leadership, or to the parental "Authority" style of leadership. Followers with this mindset only respect Autocratic leadership. So, it is important that you recognize this mindset by seeing the patterns that I am providing you in these profiles.

Mike - Bouncer

I grew up in a tougher part of town—maybe that explains why I've always felt most comfortable in situations where it's "do or die." I did well in school but was bored with it. I dropped out of college and worked as a bouncer for a few years. I enjoyed it but I wanted to make money, so I parlayed my intellect, instinct, and charisma into a successful career in mergers and acquisitions. It's a ruthless business well-suited for me—I was never shy about drawing blood. I work hard and play hard. I generally stay out of trouble though I have had a few close calls. Ask my friends and they'll tell you there's never a dull moment.

Jill - Conservative Talk Radio Host

I've hosted my own radio show for about five years now. It's a tough gig, but fortunately, I enjoy a game of hardball. Though I'm charismatic, I'm known for going for the jugular and being able to verbally dominate a caller, even if their argument is better than mine. Basically, I operate on the premise that if somebody's not strong enough to hold their own with me, they don't deserve much respect.

Sheila - Server

I learned a long time ago that power leads to getting what you want, and that a woman with sex appeal has power over most men. Today, I'm a waitress in one of the most exclusive clubs in town. I basically make a killing by pouring on the nice and, when necessary, flashing a bit of skin. But it's not just about the money, I like the feeling that I'm in control. And I like working in an atmosphere where people aren't concerned about anything but having a good time.

Autocratic Leadership

People like Sheila, Mike and Jill with this Power-centric mindset only willingly follow leaders who they respect, and they do not respect weakness.

Therefore, they tend to follow leaders who are perceived as having the most power, in other words, leaders who use an Autocratic Leadership style. Power-centric followers are motivated by power and respect, not by "people skills."

The Autocratic approach to leadership is "Unilateral" and can be summed up as follows: *impose one's will through reputation, fear and respect, tightly control information and choices, reward compliance and punish disloyalty.*

Try to recall how the world appears through the lens of an Imperial worldview.

If you perceive the world as a jungle or battlefield, then you are likely to believe the best way to advance toward your goals is always to protect yourself, gain power, and outmaneuver others who are perceived as either obedient loyalists or as obstacles, enemies or threats. Note that for autocratic leaders, both the obedient loyalists and the enemies are seen as objects to be manipulated.

If you read any of the numerous books written by former Donald Trump employees (about the man's leadership style) you will discover a textbook-accurate description of this Autocratic leadership approach.

As mentioned in an earlier chapter, bookstores are filled with popular titles that advocate this Autocratic leadership style. As I mentioned, these numerous books would not be so popular if there wasn't a market for them. I will remind you of the Stanly Bing books: *What Would Machiavelli Do? The Ends Justify the Meanness* and *Sun Tzu Was a Sissy: Conquer Your Enemies, Promote Your Friends, and Wage the Real Art of War* and the Robert Greene books *The 48 Laws of Power* and *The 50th Law*. Greene writes, "Learning the game of power requires a certain way of looking at the world, a shifting of perspective." From this autocratic perspective, everyone wants power and everyone is in a constant duplicitous game to gain more power at the expense of others.

While this autocratic style can be extremely useful on the battlefield or the oil field, unfortunately, this style has been seen on the rise even in modern countries, even in prominent leadership roles in government.

Many books (and studies) are available that provide a detailed account of the advantages and (huge) disadvantages seen when this style of leadership is deployed outside of the battlefield or oil field. Much carnage ensues.

Another excellent resource for students of Autocratic leadership, especially when it is used in the wrong context, see Harvard's Barbara Kellerman's book, *The Enablers: How Team Trump Flunked the Pandemic and Failed America.* The problem with this autocratic leadership approach is that people for whom the autocratic leadership style is their dominant style tend to be primarily or exclusively concerned with themselves and perhaps their immediate family or shareholders. Autocratic leadership simply does not work very well when those leaders have the responsibility of the wellbeing of a large diverse constituency of people whose welfare rely on wise decision-making that benefits the greater good.

However, we must never lose sight of the fact that people with a Power mindset, like Mike, Sheila and Jill in our profile examples, strongly prefer autocratic leaders.

We saw this in full effect in the United States at "Trump Rallies" in 2016-2020, and we see it anywhere a population of people with imperial worldviews feel unfairly treated and are looking for a "strongman" leader who promises to "defeat their enemies."

Most people reading this book do not have a primary Imperial worldview and therefore may find this Autocratic style of leadership unappealing, or even feel a strong aversion to it. But you must remember, everyone doesn't think like you do. Always remember that people with an Imperial worldview love autocratic leaders. In fact, they see Autocratic leadership as the only legitimate form of leadership.

Let's take a closer look at this and use our newfound "worldview lenses" to see how the other three mindsets view this Autocratic leadership style.

People who primarily identify with the Affiliative mindset (the Postmodern worldview) find the Autocratic style appalling and think such leaders should not be allowed to lead; they should be stripped of power.

People who primarily identify with the Traditional mindset believe these "power-centric" folks have lost their way and need to be "saved." In their mind, what these "lost souls" need is Jesus (or Allah depending on the culture their parents raised them in). This "save the lost souls" mentality is the basis of popular traditional programs such as the "12-Step" recovery programs which are quite useful for power-centric and traditional addicts but really risky for people with modern and postmodern worldviews.

Some Traditionals do vote for autocrats if they believe the autocrats holds their same ethnocentric beliefs, and if they believe the autocrat's claims that he will defeat their enemies. We see this with right-wing "Nationalists" movements wherever they are found. (Many examples of this have been seen in recent years, not only in the United States but also in Europe, Australia and across Asia).

However, the moment that Traditionalists recognize that the self-serving, manipulative autocrat does not actually share their traditional beliefs, they then see the same leader as immoral, and one who should be stripped of power. To invoke our familiar example from recent American history, this was seen when a subset of right-wing Republicans and gullible evangelicals realized that they had been hoodwinked, and instantly transformed from red cap-wearing MAGA loyalists to "Never Trumpers."

What about Achievers? How do they view the Autocratic leadership style?

People who primarily identify with the Achiever mindset consider the Autocratic style to be a bit extreme, but a potentially useful tool for difficult employees or suppliers that won't respond to any other tactics.

Understandably, many new students of integrally-informed approaches to leadership have difficulty imagining themselves using the Autocratic leadership style.

However, the truth is that people who primarily identify with the Power mindset are extremely unlikely to respond to the Strategic, Humanistic or Authoritarian leadership styles.

What do you do if you encounter, or manage, these Power-centric folks?

Integrally-informed leaders understand the importance of recognizing this mindset when they encounter it, and if necessary, drawing upon aspects of the Autocratic style (hopefully in judicial combination with other styles) to connect with, influence and motivate people who only respect this style. In this section, I introduced you to the key concepts of matching leadership styles to follower mindsets. Next, I want to discuss benchmarking.

Benchmarking Leadership Ability

Peter Drucker famously said, "If you can't measure it, you can't manage it." Many of the articles with titles that sound something like "why most leadership development programs fail" include this issue of measurement. Most leadership training companies use a kind of "smoke and mirrors" tactic to suggest that they measure when they actually don't. Do you know what it is?

Rather than measure the actual performance of the leaders (before and after) the training, and compare results or actual outcomes, they run bogus "participant surveys" and simply ask the participants how they "feel" about the training, are the "satisfied" with the training, and do they think they training might "benefit" their leadership. You don't have to be a PhD statistician to see how utterly bogus this approach is. What they do not do is measure actual leadership behaviors (much less leadership outcomes) before and after these programs.

You may wonder if these leadership training companies are being intentionally deceptive?

I do not think so. I've studied this problem and have become convinced that the reason they do not attempt to measure specific leadership behaviors is they <u>do not teach</u> specific leadership behaviors. Further, most leadership trainers and coaches can't even tell you what effective leadership behaviors look like, in fact, many can't even tell you what leaders actually do.

This comes back to the most fundamental problem with leadership development as it is approached today: most leadership development programs do not even recognize that leadership is a technical and complex skill, therefore they do not even attempt to break the skill down into its component parts. In an earlier example, I used basketball (dribbling, passing, shooting rebounding), baseball (batting, throwing, fielding, running the base), playing a musical instrument (notes, scales, chords, chord progressions) and mixed martial arts (wrestling, striking, grappling). Because most leadership coaching and training programs do not recognize the specific abilities, the skill sets, the techniques (behaviors), they do not teach them, and certainly have no way to measure them.

This massive failure of the leadership development industry is one of the things we must "reinvent" if we are to reform this broken $15B (per year) industry (in the U.S. and closer to $50B worldwide).

You are no doubt familiar with the "gap analysis." If we want to improve an ability, we need to have some kind of reliable measurement or benchmark to compare against and to use to develop training methods, content and evaluate progress over time.

To my knowledge, reliable proficiency benchmarks for the main areas of leadership responsibility as well as the essential leadership skills (for each), are not available anywhere beyond this book.

There are some rudimentary assessments available that I don't find adequate. There are also some very sophisticated 360 tools for evaluating leadership psychology that require significant training and an expensive certification to decipher which can be valuable but are not something that individual leaders (such as the readers of this book) can self-administer. To address an important yet unmet need,

I developed the benchmarks for the three "essential leader abilities" and the nine "leadership core competencies" drawn from more than 20,000 hours of experience researching, developing, evaluating, and training thousands of leaders over the last two decades. To keep this book short, I will refer you to my book *Accelerating Leadership* (or you can download the benchmarks for free from my website at www.AcceleratingLeadership.com).

Practice Based Leadership

I am revealing to you the exact mechanism that my partners, employees and students have been using for 22 years to get 3X to 5X better results (in terms of leadership skill improvement) over conventional leadership education practices.

It is this:

> *We teach leadership as a practice made up of concrete, specific discreet techniques. We de-emphasize concepts and we focus on the specific techniques, the practices that lead to skills, that are common to all outstanding leaders. While we do draw on best practices, we contextualize them to make sure we are using the right approach (and leadership style) with the right people and circumstances.*

It begins with treating leadership like yoga, painting, martial arts, dance or any other complex skill that practitioners deliberately practice in a very specific way.

"Deliberate practice" is the method that surgeons, professional athletes, and peak performers use to quickly learn and internalize new skills. We have used it for 20 years, helping leaders rapidly adopt new skills with consistent results.

I can summarize deliberate practice with three main ideas.

1) *You must train "technique"*

To learn a complex skill efficiently, you must isolate the skill and the techniques that make up the skill, set specific goals based on best practices and benchmarks, practice with full attention and push beyond your comfort zone.

2) *You must receive expert mentorship to do the techniques correctly*

This looks like frequent coaching and guidance from people who have mastered the technique and know how to teach it. Facilitators and coaches must be experts in the specific techniques.

3) *You must obtain feedback to calibrate and improve*

This aspect of deliberate practice involves obtaining immediate feedback (from qualified experts) to be able to calibrate and fine tune the technique as you internalize and habitualize it. The first technique has to be correct before layering on the next. And the next has to be correct before layering on the one that follows it.

This is the essence of "Practice-Based Leadership" which is the method that my partners and I pioneered 22 years ago.

I am not going to mince words here. Do not spend another dollar with so-called leadership development experts who aren't experts in the specific techniques of leadership that you need to learn to improve your skills.

You would <u>never</u> hire a guitar teacher or a baseball coach who can't play guitar or who isn't a terrific baseball player (or who doesn't know which techniques to teach you, or who talks about the "qualities" or "traits" of great guitar or baseball players). Don't hire leadership trainers or coaches who do that either!

To break it down further into the techniques, you wouldn't go into a baseball "batting cage" to train on that skill with someone who is a "mindset coach" or "life coach" or "executive coach" who has never swung a bat (much less possesses the expert level proficiency of doing the technique perfectly).

Imagine a martial arts or baseball coach who only talked to you about mindset and asked you a lot of reflection questions but didn't teach you how to correctly practice your new techniques, or worse, didn't even know the techniques in the first place?

Kind of obvious when you think about it, right?

Repetition is the mother of skill. So, I will repeat this crucial point.

> *The only effective way to learn technical and complex skills (baseball, basketball, playing a musical instrument, martial arts, flying an airplane or leadership) is to break the ability down into its component parts or "skill sets" and then train, memorize and internalize each of those techniques until they become second nature.*

Learning complex skills follows a pattern that looks like this. Again, you already know this because you have already mastered numerous complex skills. So let me remind you what you already know.

Over many weeks, practices become habits. Over many months, habits become skills. With time and ongoing practice, those skills combine into "skill sets." Ultimately, the skill sets come together to form the "ability" (the complex skill) that the learner is practicing.

To be competent at baseball, an athlete must have the skills to throw, catch, hit and run. To be competent at MMA, an athlete must have wrestling, kickboxing, and grappling skills.

For the past 22+ years, all of my leadership trainings have used "Deliberate Practice" principles from "Expert Performance Theory." This is central to why my leadership trainings consistently produce results where most leadership training programs fail.

Two decades ago, I was the first to apply *Expert Performance Theory* and *Deliberate Practice* to leadership development at Integral Institute (where I was a senior faculty member) and the Stagen Leadership Academy (that I co-founded) when I created the original "Integral Leadership Program." That program is still running 22 years later (and still going strong).

As pioneers in this practice-based approach to leadership development, is safe to say that my partners and I have more experience than anyone else in the world with it.

We literally invented the category of "practice based leadership."

I have personally spent 20 hours a week, 50 weeks a year for over 20 years training, mentoring, and coaching leaders, totaling around 1,000 hours per year. The "10,000 hour rule," popularized by Malcolm Gladwell's book "Outliers," suggests that it takes about 10,000 hours for someone to become an expert or master a complex skill such as medicine, martial arts, management, or leadership. I have logged more than 10,000 hours *training leaders* and additional 10,000 hours *coaching leaders*, for a total of over 20,000 hours. This provides me with a breadth of relevant experience and depth of understanding of leadership development that very few people have.

I am not telling you this to impress you. I am telling you this to impress upon you that the information in this book is coming from someone who has vast experience using these methods and who is a legitimate "expert" as defined by Expert Performance Theory. I am telling you this in the hopes of motivating and inspiring you to adopt these methods and use them in your own leadership development and in your organization.

These methods work, and they work better than most of the other leadership development methods you are likely to encounter.

All of this experience has led me to one crucial conclusion: *the only effective way to learn the complex skill we call leadership is to use a technique- and practice-based approach.*

This insight and this belief flies in the face of convention.

Approximately 80-90% of the leadership training programs on the market focus on character traits, abstract "qualities" of leaders, and vague concepts like "EQ" yet offer no specific techniques or skills to practice to develop emotional intelligence. (More on EQ later.)

The straight truth is this: To learn complex skills, especially leadership, you need training on individual techniques and then you must practice those techniques until they become internalized, and then over time, combine those growing skills together to form new abilities.

The phrase "10,000 hours" is likely familiar to many readers, but few know its origins. It was popularized by Malcom Gladwell in his book *Outliers*: *The Story of Success,* but the term was originally coined by Anders Ericsson, who researched and developed the method called "Deliberate Practice." Ericsson's research showed that only certain types of practice lead to high-performance or expert-level skills, not all practice.

When you leverage this method called "deliberate practice" in our management and leadership skill learning efforts, you can expect to dramatically increase the rate at which you can level up abilities. And while it could take 5-10 years to achieve that 10,000 hour "expert" level performance in leadership skills, we can expect massive gains in performance in just half a year to a year if you follow the guidelines that "expert performance theory" and this book explain.

My experience shows that following my Accelerating Leadership method (which in my programs includes micro learning tutorial videos and weekly group coaching on Zoom), a leader can go from beginner to intermediate, or intermediate to expert in only about 6-12 months. If you apply all the things you are learning in this book series (all four books), even without the benefit of my micro-learning tutorial videos and my group coaching on Zoom, you could still go from beginner to intermediate or intermediate to expert level in just a couple of years.

There is an old saying that goes, "Practice makes perfect".

Like so many old sayings, this one points to something true and useful, but isn't really accurate. Sure, practice is important and certainly helpful. But if you are practicing in any way other than the perfect "form" then that is actually reinforcing wrong technique.

Learning the wrong form of a technique is hardly what any reasonable person would call "makes perfect".

So, we can correct that misconception by restating it this way... *Perfect practice makes perfect.*

This idea of "perfect practice" is not just a figure of speech. Nor does it point merely to the correct form of a technique mentioned previously. "Perfect practice" is about a very specific type of practice that dramatically accelerates learning and crushes the steep learning curves associated with complex skills.

While this relatively new kind of "practice" is starting to gain popularity, most people have either never heard of it, or have perhaps heard of it but don't know how to engage it and use it.

As mentioned prior, the person who pioneered much of the research in this area and coined the term "Deliberate Practice" was Anders Ericsson. He has written several books, but I will highlight two here.

They are: *The Cambridge Handbook of Expertise and Expert Performance* and *Peak: Secrets from the New Science of Expertise.*

Ericsson's research suggests that only certain types of practice can lead to expertise. George Leonard also described a similar concept in his book: *Mastery: The Keys to Success and Long-Term Fulfillment.* I will use Anders Ericsson's own words to define and clarify exactly what deliberate practice is...

> *"Deliberate practice develops skills that other people have already figured out how to do and for which effective training techniques have been established. The practice regimen should be designed and overseen by a teacher or coach who is familiar with the abilities of expert performers and with how those abilities can best be developed."*

Ericsson found that surgeons, for example, use deliberate practice, which involves specific goals and immediate feedback. Surgeons can see how their actions impact their patient's health and make improvements quickly.

Radiologists, on the other hand, don't have the same connection between their diagnosis and the outcome (the long-term health of their patients). While this example highlights the critical importance of specific goals and feedback, Ericsson strongly emphasizes that it's not enough to merely mirror the behaviors of the experts.

It's important to understand the thinking, the reasoning and the feelings behind those behaviors. In plain terms, it's not enough to just parrot behaviors that would be how the behavior looks from the outside. You must also understand how that technique feels from the inside. What does the expert, the exemplar, think and feel when they are performing the technique?

Ericsson's research showed that the quality of these internal representations separates experts from novices. This applies to every field they have studied, including rock climbing, music, sports, research, writing, memory skills, and sales.

It's important to note that you cannot create optimal "internal representations" (how the technique is experienced from the inside) just by doing an activity over and over again. Rather, you need to model the internal representations of an exemplar who has the skill you want to acquire. This is why I will frequently remind you throughout this book that the fastest way to learn leadership skills is to get mentoring, guidance and coaching from people who are experts in those specific techniques.

To truly understand a skill, it's not enough to just hear about it or read about it, you must experience it and practice it over and over until it becomes habit. This is one of the main reasons that most leadership development programs fail to develop leader. They usually teach the wrong things in the wrong way. If they aren't teaching specific skills then they aren't actually helping people get better at the technical and complex skill called leadership.

To progress in your leadership skills, your facilitators and coaches must be experts in both the techniques they are teaching and the best methods to teach those techniques. If their "leadership model" does not emphasize specific techniques and practices, and if their advice to help leaders get better at the technical and complex skill of leadership does not incorporate "deliberate practice," then I strongly suggest you look elsewhere.

Further, if your leadership trainer or coach is not a "black belt" (an expert) in the techniques they are coaching you in, then they are not qualified to coach you.

You must get this.

> *If you spend money on leadership coaches who are not experts in the specific skills of leadership, then you are wasting your time and your money. And this includes the ubiquitous "mindset coaches" who will happily take your money but can't teach you anything about leadership. People who say "mindset is everything" don't know much about anything. Mindset is most definitely not everything. Its not even the main thing. Mindset is 20% at most. Strategy and technique is 80% or more of what leads to success in any endeavor.*

Mindset coaching is mainly helpful for people <u>who already know how to do a technique perfectly</u> and they are trying to adopt the best psychology (mindset) to help them do it more consistently. Mindset coaching is great for professional athletes who are already at the very top of their game and who know the techniques well.

Executive coaches and self-described leadership coaches who focus primarily on mindset, in my experience, do this because the do not know the strategies, skills or techniques of leadership.

In my opinion, if they did know the techniques of leadership, they would be sharing them with their clients (a lot more than mindset). To be blunt, focusing on mindset is a primary way that unqualified leadership coaches cover up their lack of knowledge about leadership. Do them a favor and share this book with them. Maybe they will choose to level up their knowledge about leadership.

As mentioned earlier in this book, leadership advice-givers can't agree on a single definition of effective leadership because they have different worldviews and as such, see different approaches (or styles) of leadership as more appealing (based on the values, assumptions and beliefs inherent in their specific worldview). I spent over a decade working with Ken Wilber at Integral Institute and my R&D team at Stagen Leadership Academy, and more than a million of dollars developing and testing the "Unifying Theory of Leadership" that provides the theoretical foundation for this work.

This short book summarizes the resulting breakthroughs in understanding leadership, instructional design for leadership training programs, and strategies for rapidly raising effective leadership skills. This book discloses this well-kept trade secret, which we've used for nearly two decades to train over 10,000 corporate executives (and many leaders in developing countries through my nonprofit organization).

I hope you can appreciate the value of the research, frameworks, models and tools that you now hold in your hands. I have spent well over a million dollars of my own money, and many millions of dollars of my company's money over a twenty-year period in order to now be in a position to bring you the "simplicity on the other side of complexity" reflected in this model.

I spent five years working with Ken Wilber and Integral Institute to create the original *Unifying Theory of Leadership*. I spent ten additional years testing the model with corporate leaders, simplifying and refining it, resulting in my *Leadership Rosetta Stone*. Then I spent another five years expanding the testing beyond the corporate world to also include international humanitarian efforts, governments, military leaders, religious and even tribal and indigenous leaders in third-world countries, culminating in the *Universal Leadership Model* presented in this book (and my other books).

I tell you this not to impress you; rather, to impress upon you the real value contained in this book that you now own, and hopefully to inspire you to learn, internalize, and most importantly, put into practice these extremely valuable academically-sound, time-tested methods.

In this book, I provide a sufficient overview of the practice based approach for you to apply in your leadership development efforts (in the "Execution & Performance" dimension of leadership).

If you want to learn more about this methodology, please see my book, *Accelerating Leadership: The Groundbreaking Method for Rapid Leadership Development That Achieves Twice the Results in Half the Time at a Fraction of the Cost.*

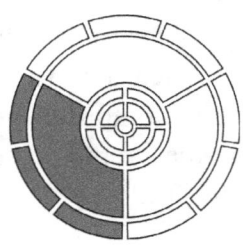

CHAPTER 5: BENCHMARKING EXECUTION & PERFORMANCE LEADERSHIP CAPACITY

In the "Accelerating Leadership Framework" presented previously, I briefly introduced you to this area of responsibility that all leaders share. In this next part of the book, we will take a deeper dive into this dimension, and unpack these three essential skill sets leaders use to fulfill these responsibilities.

First, in this short chapter, I will provide you benchmarks for this "overall dimension" of leadership that I call "Execution & Performance." So, these benchmarks are "high level" for the whole "essential ability" as I also call this dimension. Recall that there are three dimensions of leadership. These were all three summarized previously and I have published one book per dimension. Before we move on to subsequent chapters, where we drill down into each "skill set" in this dimension, it is important to establish benchmarks for this overall "capacity" for "Execution & Performance" (as I call it).

Also, you will find that in subsequent chapters (one per skill set), I will also provide benchmarks for each of the discrete "skill sets" that leaders utilize in this dimension. Those benchmarks will be more granular (per skill set) as contrasted with this high-level view of a leader's proficiency in the overall "essential ability" we refer to as "Execution & Performance."

Consider assessing how you "measure up" against these established benchmarks. Keep in mind that, statistically speaking, most people tend to fall within the middle range of a typical "bell curve". Therefore, most readers of this book will likely fall somewhere in the "intermediate" range of proficiency in this essential ability, the dimension I call "Execution & Performance." If you were to fall in the lower range, then you have some immediate work to do to avoid undermining your leadership credibility.

My hope is that, after reading this book, adopting the best practices outlined here, and engaging in these activities in your leadership role with your team for several months, you will begin to see your proficiency level improve from "intermediate" to "late intermediate." And with a few more months of practice, I hope that you will progress into the "early advanced" level of proficiency.

Over time, if you socialize these practices with your team, it is possible to get your whole team to reach the "advanced" (or "higher levels") of proficiency in this essential ability that I am calling Execution & Performance.

Once you move into the next chapters on the more granular specific skill sets, it is more likely that you will find one in which you (or members of your team or certain teams) fall into the lower range. But let's not get ahead of ourselves. Let's take a moment and get grounded in this essential leadership ability called Execution & Performance. (Recall that earlier I also called these three dimensions the "Inherent Leadership Responsibilities." So let's take an honest look at how your leadership measures up in this essential leadership ability and this inherent responsibility.

Definition

First let's define. The essential leadership ability that I am calling *Culture & Teamwork* includes all of the activities related to establishing roles and responsibilities, identifying and closing performance gaps, planning and managing projects using the appropriate tools to coordinate work across teams, and maintaining high productivity so that organizational resources are used efficiently to achieve shared goals in the desired time frames.

It is helpful to orient our thinking about this crucial dimension of leadership by reviewing some of the key questions, challenges, and goals that leaders have when addressing this area of leadership.

Execution & Performance Questions

- How can we hold people accountable and identify and close performance gaps so that expectations are consistently met?

- How can we coordinate the people and efforts (objectives, workstreams, timelines) so that our projects are consistently implemented successfully on time and on a budget?

- How can we make sure work is completed in a productive, organized, focused, efficient and effective way (in challenging environments, including working remotely often with lots of distractions and competing commitments)?

Execution & Performance Challenges

The following are common challenges leaders report in this dimension.

- Managers wearing too many hats / managers have "too much to do" with too few resources.

- Leaders have multiple competing priorities and feel overwhelmed with an unrealistic workload

- Lack of follow-through or lack of accountability by individuals, teams or departments

- Unclear or poorly communicated expectations from boss, therefore, expectations often not met

- Department or organization is understaffed and lacks sufficient resources, we must do more with less

- Missing milestones and deadlines due to poor project management (or unrealistic expectations)

- Poor quality, sloppy work, disappointing results, unhappy customers

- Delegation is not happening well or consistently (not clear, not realistic) and lack of follow through

- Difficulty with group decision-making, when decisions are made, they are often met with resistance

- Managers lack the authority to make decisions necessary to achieve outcomes

- Confusion or lack of clarity about roles, responsibilities and who has what authority

- Inadequate project planning, projects are not well-defined, work streams lack clarity or accountability

Execution & Performance Goals

The following are common goals leaders report in this dimension.

- Clarify roles for all team members so people know what activities and outcomes are expected of them

- Help a team member who is struggling to close a performance gap

- Get better at holding people accountable, create a "culture of accountability"

- Get better at planning and managing projects using the appropriate tools to coordinate people and effort

- Assess and upgrade existing meetings, upgrade and enhance with current best practices

- Level up our time management practices to handle calendars and schedules better

Precision Proficiency Benchmarking

A leader's skill proficiency in any of these dimensions is determined less by looking at the leader, a better gauge of the leader's proficiency is to look at the results observed in the organization. Therefore, on the following pages you will find the benchmarks to use when evaluating a leader and their team or organization's current capability in this dimension. These organizational benchmarks are very helpful to use when asking members of a team to self-assess the team's current capabilities. Not only does this provide valuable insights to the leaders, but it also is a terrific conversation starter that you can use to discuss this aspect of the team's (or department or organization's) strengths and gaps which could be elevated to support the group's ability to achieve its shared objectives.

Lower Range

A leader and a team functioning in the lower range of proficiency in this skill set might describe it this way:

We have some obvious gaps in execution and accountability. Our team doesn't know much about time and task management. We hear complaints that meetings are viewed as ineffective. Our people manage their projects with simple tools such as Post-it notes or spreadsheets (no shared dashboards or software being used). Beyond obligatory annual performance reviews, ongoing expectations, accountability and performance are rarely discussed openly.

Intermediate Range

A leader and a team functioning in the middle range of proficiency in this skill set might describe it this way:

We execute sometimes, but we are inconsistent. Some team members have strong productivity skills, while others don't. Some members have formal "project management" training and use dashboards to coordinate efforts, but these tools have not been adopted by the whole team. We try to make responsibilities and expectations explicit. Still, we don't do regular check-ins to identify and address performance gaps. Accountability conversations, when they happen, are often awkward.

Higher Range

A leader and a team functioning in the higher range of proficiency in this skill set might describe it this way:

We really "execute" quite well. Most team members stay focused, efficient and productive. Several of our managers have prior project management experience and have helped us institutionalize disciplined project planning and follow-through habits (with shared dashboards, frequent check-ins, and so on). Missed milestones are rare. We have clear responsibilities and expectations, and we are comfortable calling out and learning from the occasional "accountability breakdown."

Now that you have grounded in the levels of proficiency (low, intermediate and high) in this overall dimension, we will move into the subsequent chapters, one per skill set, and we will review the benchmarks for those specific skill sets and many of the most important and most helpful skills, techniques, tools and practices that bolster a leaders ability in each of these skill sets. The first skill set is "Performance Management."

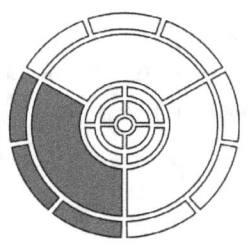

CHAPTER 6: PERFORMANCE MANAGEMENT

First we begin with a clear definition and the benchmarks for levels of proficiency in this skill set. I define this skill set by saying, "Performance Management involves managing performance so that responsibilities, expectations, and agreements are consistently met, including ongoing accountability conversations to manage commitments and breakdowns when expectations are not met."

Team Discussion

When you initiate a conversation with your employees and team(s), you could use some version of the following questions.

- How do we identify and close expectation gaps?

- How do we manage performance so that responsibilities, expectations, and agreements are consistently met?

- How do we approach accountability conversations?

- How do we manage commitments and what do we do when expectations are not met?

Benchmarks

Next, we move into the benchmarks for this skill set.

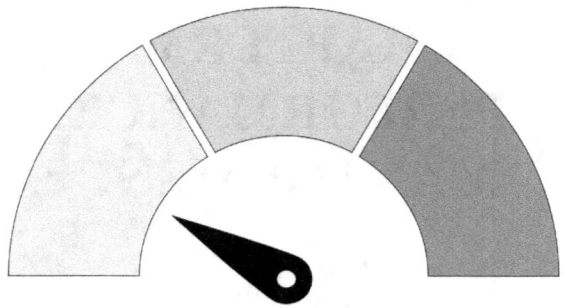

PERFORMANCE MANAGEMENT LOWER RANGE

A leader and a team functioning in the lower range of proficiency in this skill set might describe it this way.

We have annual performance reviews; between those, each manager attempts to manage expectations with employees informally. We have not conducted any training on how to have accountability conversations. Deadlines are often missed, and performance is inconsistent. Overall, there are a lot of unmet expectations and disappointing performances.

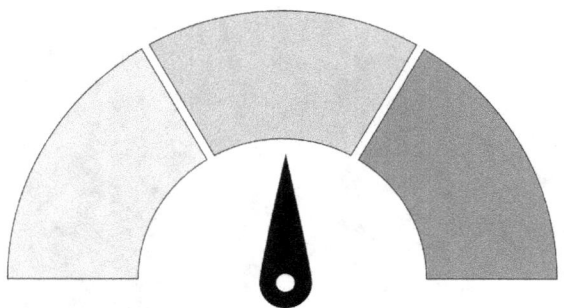

PERFORMANCE MANAGEMENT INTERMEDIATE RANGE

A leader and a team functioning in the middle range of proficiency in this skill set might describe it this way.

Between annual performance reviews, we have regular quarterly check-ins, we make responsibilities and expectations explicit, and we try to hold each other accountable. However, we have not institutionalized formal training and tools, and some team members have difficulty holding others accountable. Therefore, accountability and overall performance are a little spotty across the organization, and expectations are frequently not met.

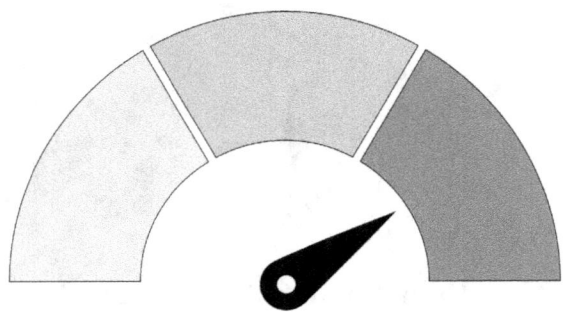

PERFORMANCE MANAGEMENT HIGHER RANGE

A leader and a team functioning in the higher range of proficiency in this skill set might describe it this way.

Our organization has advanced performance management systems in place. We have clear responsibilities, expectations and agreements. We have quarterly check-ins with our direct support staff to give them feedback and support them toward their annual developmental goals. Our team members are proactive about ongoing performance conversations, including having regular "accountability conversations" to manage commitments, and calling out and learning from "accountability breakdowns" when expectations are occasionally unmet.

RESPONSIBILITY, AUTHORITY, AND EXPECTATIONS

Responsibility, authority, and expectations are fundamental aspects of leadership. In this section, i will introduce new ways to think about these important dimensions of leadership, as well as new approaches that you and your team can use to elevate your collective performance.

Responsibility

Responsibility is possessing the "ability" to "respond" within a duty, obligation or requirement to take action.

Your responsibilities are the areas in which you use your "abilities" for "responding" to the needs associated with your role. Take a moment to reflect on the job description of your role.

Can you name your top five responsibilities?

Now think of the men and women who report to you. Consider each of them and each one's role. Do you think if you asked them to list their top 5 responsibilities, they would say the same things that you would say if you listed their top responsibilities?

While job descriptions offer some guidance for responsibilities, much of the time, employees have a different idea of what they are responsible for than their boss.

In this and other sections, we will explore the value of gaining clarity and alignment on what each person (in each role) is responsible for. Also, consider the things for which you feel responsible each month and each week. And think of the men and women who report to you. What are they responsible for each week and each month?

Again, do you feel that there is a tight alignment between their idea of responsibilities and yours? Is this something that you regularly discuss with them, or is this something that you simply assume that they fully understand and that they are fully aligned with you?

Some of your main responsibilities are made explicit by your boss and perhaps outlined in writing in your job description. Similarly, some of the responsibilities of the men and women who report to you are explicit, while others may simply be implied.

As a leader, you may also feel responsible for many other things that may not be explicitly mentioned in your job description.

Leaders take responsibility. Oftentimes, leaders feel responsible for many things not explicitly stated in their job description.

Authority

Authority is quite different from responsibility, and it is very helpful for leaders and followers to understand the difference.

Authority is the "right to make decisions, allocate resources, and give orders."

There are two areas of resources that the authority operates on: bandwidth and budget. Bandwidth involves the human resources of people's time and attention.

Budget consists of the organization's financial resources, including the mobilization of assets and equipment. Additionally, authority grants power and sets expectations for the men and women who report to you.

As you may have already intuited, it can be a real problem when people are going to be held responsible for certain outcomes, yet they do not have the authority to make decisions (and allocate resources) to achieve those outcomes.

Take a moment to reflect. What authority do you have?

What decisions are you authorized to make on your own, in your role, without approval from the person you report to?

What resources do you manage?

What orders can you make, and to whom?

These are some of the things you have the authority to do.

When authority and responsibility work together with clarity, teams are able to work effectively and smoothly.

For a team and an organization to be effective, it is important to have clearly defined roles with explicit responsibilities and a clear understanding of authority.

This results in your and your teams' ability to coordinate collective efforts effectively and achieve desired outcomes consistently.

Three Common Challenges

In organizational life, we see three common challenges that we want to address in this section.

1. People and teams are sometimes given responsibilities but may not be empowered adequately to fulfill those responsibilities.

Being asked to do something that you do not know how to do, have not been trained for, and lack skill in executing is an obvious problem for the person receiving the assignment.

Be on the lookout for the difficult situation when responsibilities are delegated, along with specific work assignments, yet there may be a gap between what the person is able to do and has the resources to do, and what is being asked of them.

2. People often function with responsibilities and authorities that are not adequately aligned.

Another common challenge is when people are held responsible for outcomes even though they have not been given the appropriate authority to allocate resources and make decisions that would be required to achieve those outcomes.

It can be demoralizing if a person feels responsible for an outcome but does not have the necessary authority to make key decisions, set expectations, mobilize needed resources and give orders necessary to accomplish that outcome.

This is usually not something that is obvious. It requires a leader who is paying attention and listening to his or her people to identify these "misalignments".

3. Individuals and teams sometimes have authorities that cross over or interfere with each other.

As an organization grows, and as conditions change over time, people may have the authority to influence situations, yet those decisions and efforts may cross or interfere with one another. Even though managers and leaders may have good intentions, conflicts can arise when efforts are thwarted, interfered with, or valuable resources are wasted.

It is important to be on the lookout for authority that may cross over or interfere between roles, people, functions, and departments.

Expectations

Expectations hold an organization together.

There are many explicit and implicit expectations coursing through your organization every day, week, month and year. These expectations can change over time, just like the ebb and flow of the ocean tide. They may shift as people get promoted, as roles and objectives evolve, or as the environment changes.

Continually clarifying expectations can be thought of as "organizational hygiene." If we don't keep our expectations tidy and clean, problems will eventually arise in the form of misunderstandings, conflict, missed deadlines and objectives, tension, frustration and even loss of credibility and trust.
Within each of the three common challenges identified, expectations are at the root of the problem. Either the expectations are unstated, unclear, misunderstood or misaligned in some way.

Understanding and clarifying expectations is critical for your success as a leader and for the success of the men and women and teams who report to you.

There is a saying, "An ounce of prevention is worth a pound of cure". This is very applicable to expectations.

When we do not invest adequate time upfront in clarifying expectations, we end up spending even more time addressing avoidable problems that unclear expectations cause.

We want to highlight two specific kinds of expectations: explicit and implicit.

Explicit expectations are expectations that have been clearly communicated, understood by all parties, and agreed upon.

Explicit expectations are what people can be effectively held accountable to.

Implicit expectations are held in people's minds, but may not be clearly expressed. Because they have not been explicitly communicated, they have rarely been agreed to by other parties.

In fact, much of the time, other parties are not even aware of the expectations, making them challenging to effectively manage.

If you do not directly express an expectation, and confirm that the other person understands it the same way you do, then you may have difficulty holding them accountable as the project unfolds or as time goes by.

It is your responsibility to communicate the precise expectations you have with all of the people who report to you.

If you are committed to achieving the outcomes for which you're responsible, then you should challenge and support the people around you with explicit expectations.

Aligning Responsibility and Authority

As mentioned previously, problems often occur when people are held responsible for outcomes where they do not have the appropriate authority to influence those outcomes.

People feel empowered when they have the ability to influence events toward the outcomes they are expected to achieve and are responsible to deliver.

This increases engagement, morale, motivation, and job satisfaction.

Alternatively, it can be demoralizing if a person feels responsible for an outcome but does not have the authority to allocate resources (bandwidth and budget) to ensure that the outcome is achieved.

Put simply, if people are going to have responsibilities, they must also have the necessary authorities to make decisions and allocate resources to fulfill those responsibilities.

Ideally, each area of work should have one role that is responsible for a set of weekly and monthly activity outcomes while also having the authority to make the decisions needed to mobilize the resources necessary to achieve those outcomes.

One of the best ways to clarify details about a person's authority, especially for managers, is to make lists of every decision that they are authorized to make.

Roles

Roles are often underdeveloped in many civilian, government and military environments. The role description may be high-level or abstract and may not offer the details of the weekly and monthly activities and the outcomes that are expected of the person fulfilling that role.

We can think of roles as "organizational positions." By clarifying each role in your organization (department, unit or team), you can become more precise in where you locate each person in relation to others. When clarifying roles, try to add more explicit detail about the activities and outcomes the person in that role is responsible for, and try to make the expectations as explicit as possible.

Good role formation and role clarity come from recognizing the work that is needed to be done in specific terms.

You and your team know the territories of your work better than just about anyone else. As a result, leaders often benefit by using their teams to help them identify all of the areas of work they collectively operate in.

Ideally, each major area of work should have someone whose role is primarily responsible for that work. This role is responsible for this particular area's set of ongoing activities and desired outcomes (each week, month and year).

Each role should also have the necessary authority to make the decisions and allocate resources to achieve those outcomes.

You likely already have many established roles in the main areas of work. But it is a good idea to do an "audit" of these roles and their responsibilities, activities, outcomes and the authority vested in each role to make decisions and allocate resources to achieve those outcomes.

If there have been any recent changes in organizational roles (such as promotions or new hires), or if the organizational objectives or external demands on the organization have shifted in recent months or years, it's possible that you may identify gaps or areas of misalignment.

While the dynamic nature of responsibility, authority and expectations over time can be a challenge for even the best leaders, the important takeaway is for you to continually steer towards greater clarity and alignment.

Over time, you and your team will be more empowered when you've established more clarity on your team's roles.

Everyone will be more aligned on their respective responsibility and authority and the team will be operating with more explicit expectations.

When roles are calibrated and maintained well, your team will also feel less stressed and more empowered.

You will know you are tracking well when your team trusts each other's roles and each person spends most of their time focusing on their best efforts for their area of work.

In subsequent sections of this book, we'll give you additional tools to enhance your team's decision-making, communication, and ability to hold one another accountable.

Accountability Fundamentals

In this section, we are going to work with the crucial practice of accountability. Accountability is a skill that both managers and employees should enhance. Organizations committed to effectiveness and what is often called "execution" must cultivate a culture of accountability.

The essence of accountability as a "practice" is increasing awareness of what people actually say and do, and the implications of those statements and actions.

Organizational consultant Mark Youngblood uses the term "Committed Action" for the practice of accountability. He describes the essence of this practice as "making and keeping promises". He has observed that where commitment is absent, performance always suffers.

Employees throughout the organization are making commitments to each other every day.

Many of the challenges that managers face stem from broken or poorly crafted commitments.

All too often, people fail to consider the fact that in order to actually deliver on a commitment, they may need to solicit and oversee a fairly complex set of supporting actions and agreements from other team members.

Donald Sull, the author of the Harvard Business Review article entitled *"Promise-Based Management"*, outlines five characteristics of good commitments that support accountability.

Good Commitments Are Public.

Agreements that are made, monitored, and completed in public are more binding — and therefore more desirable — than side deals hammered out in private.

When individuals make commitments out in the open, in front of their peers and bosses, they can't conveniently forget what they agreed to do.

Good Commitments Are Active.

Negotiating a commitment should be an active, collaborative process that takes place through dialogue. Active conversations probe assumptions and should comprise offers, counteroffers, commitments, and even refusals. Good commitments are voluntary.

The most effective agreements are not coerced, but voluntary, and the parties have a viable option (such as a counteroffer) for saying something other than an unqualified yes.

People assume less responsibility for promises made under threat (although they may comply out of fear). By contrast, most people feel deeply obliged to follow through on a commitment if they exercise free will in making it.

Good Commitments are Mission- and Values-Based.

Commitments are often solicited without tying them explicitly to either the organization's goals (or values) or individual goals (or values).

Making the connection to the organization's aims helps individuals contextualize their commitment and feel integral to the success of the organization.

Tying commitments to personal values taps individuals' intrinsic motivations and fosters a greater sense of meaning and purpose.

Good Commitments are Specific and Explicit.

This last point cannot be emphasized enough. All parties must be specific and explicit about what their commitments throughout the entire commitment life cycle are going to look like.

Requests must be clear from the start, progress reports should accurately reflect how promises are being executed, and successes (or failures) should be outlined in detail. In the sections that follow, we will learn how we can become more disciplined about how we make requests, make commitments, and follow up on those commitments. And we will explore ways that we can learn from the inevitable missed targets and communication breakdowns that can occur.

Accountability Conversations

The essence of the skill of accountability is the way we make requests, make commitments, and manage those commitments.

It really boils down to being precise and disciplined in the way we talk about accountability. Some managers try to take a kind of "legalistic" orientation toward commitments, defining them according to the terms of a deal, much as lawyers might focus on specific clauses in a contract. While this might be appropriate for a vendor whom you are holding accountable to a contract, this is not the appropriate tone to take with a team member.

According to Fred Kofman, the author of the book "*Conscious Business*," our discussions related to accountability occur on three different levels (or topics) that we can highlight here.

1. The Work to Be Done

The first level involves the task itself (including the broader project and work involved). Every commitment has a task implication. Accountability involves a complex network of commitments to get things done that an individual could not achieve alone.

2. The Relationship

The second level involves the relationship, and especially the trust between the two parties. As such, every commitment has relationship implications.

3. An Individual's Credibility

Kofman argues that, on the deepest level, the way people approach commitments informs and defines their credibility on the team. "How good is your word?" he asks. "Do people view you as a person they can rely on to keep their commitments?"

Four Elements of Accountability Conversations Practice

There are five keys to accountability that we will focus on in this book.

1. Making Effective Requests
3. Committed Responses
4. Managing Commitments
5. Managing and Learning from "Breakdowns"

Making Effective Requests

Many people are under the impression that their requests are clear and are surprised to learn later that the expectations implicit in their requests were not met.

Do you hear exchanges like the following in your organization?

"Someone needs to work on that managers' report."
"Yes, you're right." "We need the managers' report for the meeting next week."
"Good idea." "We've got to get going on that report."
"Yeah."

Interactions like these can be deceiving. It sounds like something productive occurred, but actually this is far from the case. These example statements are not effective requests, and the example responses are certainly not commitments. To establish clear conditions for satisfaction, ask the following questions;

What exactly do I want (or need)? Under what conditions would I be satisfied?

How will I know if my concern is resolved?

What would be happening or what would stop happening if my concern were resolved?

Bear in mind that not every detail needs to be articulated at the start of a project, but it is important to be as specific as possible and then amend the agreement as more details become available. The key point is to be able to leave the conversation with the conditions of satisfaction stated as clearly as possible and understood and agreed to by all relevant parties. Following are good examples of effective requests (contrasted with ineffective examples).

Ineffective Request: "Someone needs to work on the managers' report."

Effective Request: "Andy, I need the managers' report by noon tomorrow so I can prepare for a meeting. Will you complete it by then and leave it on my desk?"

Ineffective Request: "I'd like to get a copy of those sales figures."

Effective Request: "Jon, I need your team's sales figures by the end of the day today so I can begin strategizing for Q2. Will you send them to me by email?"

Committed Responses

Following are some familiar examples of responses that would not qualify as commitments. Do any of these vague, non-committed responses sound familiar to you?

I should be able to get that done. I'm working on it.

Yeah, we should talk about that. We could do that.

Don't worry. No problem.

When I get around to it. I'll see what I can do. It shouldn't be a problem. That's a good idea.

Let's see what happens. Sounds good to me.

I'll do my best. I'll try.

I'll check into it. I'll look at it after I get more information.

Clearly, none of these responses could be categorized as commitments. Regardless of the clarity of an "effective request", if the reply sounds like one of the examples listed, then there is no commitment (and therefore nothing to be held accountable for). At some point or another, everyone fails to keep commitments—this cannot be avoided entirely.

Yet the skill with which these commitments are managed can have a significant impact on the ability to execute successfully (individually, in teams, and organizationally). Keeping commitments affects others' perception of your professionalism and their willingness to trust you. Would your co-workers and employees say that you keep your promises?

If not, how has that impacted your effectiveness and your relationships?

Before you make a commitment, consider the following.

1. Do I really intend to do this?
2. Do I know how to do this?
3. Do I have the resources to do this?

The Four Kinds of Committed Responses

"Committed Responses," as we call them, fall into one of the following four categories. Anything outside of these four kinds of responses would not be considered an actual commitment.

No (Sorry, I can't commit to that)

When someone says no to something, bandwidth is created to say yes to something else. Yet saying no can be difficult—people may procrastinate or avoid giving a definitive answer to a request. Although it may be slightly uncomfortable to do so, declining a request can actually build trust in a relationship. It reinforces the fact that a person doesn't commit to tasks he isn't serious about following through on. Example: "No, I'm not going to be able to attend that meeting."

Yes (I Commit)

Say yes only if the intention is truly there to complete the task, if you are actually able to do it, and if the resources are available. Rather than just saying yes, restate the specific request in your response.

Example: "Yes, I will complete that report and send it to you by Wednesday at 5 p.m." Promise to Promise. People often need some time to carefully consider the request (and their intentions, abilities, and resources) before making a commitment.

If you can't answer yes at the time the request is made, then commit to responding at a specific later time. Example:

"I'll get back to you with an answer by noon on Friday."

Counteroffer (Negotiate)

When you determine you cannot fulfill a request (or offer) as proposed unless certain conditions of satisfaction are altered, you can make a "counteroffer". In other words, you can negotiate the terms of the commitment so that it is something you can actually commit to. Example: "Although I can't get the report to you by Wednesday, I can commit to having it to you by the end of the day on Friday."

Managing Commitments

It is necessary to check in regularly (appropriate to the timing of the project or initiative) to ensure the action matches the conditions for satisfaction.

This allows enough time to "course correct" or to clarify the conditions of the agreement as time passes, more information surfaces, obstacles arise, or our understanding of the circumstances change.

These check-ins can be included as regular agenda items for the rhythm meetings used in project management, often making it easier to surface the productive conflict of needing to change a previously promised commitment before the original deadline gets close or passes.

Canceling Requests

In the practice of accountability, the person who makes the request is expected to formally cancel (in a timely fashion) if the work is no longer needed based on a changing context.

This avoids an unnecessary waste of time and effort.

When canceling a request or offer, it is helpful to provide the specific reasons for the cancellation, so the other person can appreciate how the circumstances have shifted rather than bring negative assumptions to bear on the person originally making the request.

Revoking Commitments

People often ignore or duck promises they aren't going to keep, hoping the other person won't notice or call them on it. Over time, this behavior can damage trust and relationships.

To avoid this, it is essential to revoke a commitment as soon as you realize it will be impossible to fulfill it. Again, provide specific reasons so others can appreciate how the circumstances have shifted.

Revoking a commitment can be uncomfortable and difficult to do. It's human nature to prefer to avoid the issue and pretend as if everything will be fine.

However, sincerely revoking a commitment can actually build trust by showing the other person that they doesn't have to wonder if the commitment will be honored. The other person will know she'll be notified in advance if the terms of the agreement can't be met.

Accountability Breakdown Conversations

When requests and responses are vague and ineffective, there's no commitment to breaking. If no actual commitment has been made, then there is nothing to hold someone accountable to. Therefore, there can be no "breakdown" in the commitment. For example, if a person agrees to complete a task but does not commit to a specific date, a breakdown cannot be declared.

It is only when a real commitment is established that the possibility of a breakdown arises.

An interesting dynamic begins to occur when genuine commitments are made. People begin to notice everything that is inconsistent with that commitment. Given this dynamic, once real commitments are made, occasional breakdowns can and should be expected. Indeed, it is the nature of organizational life that intentions are not always met, and milestones are not always completed by agreed-upon dates.

Accountability practitioners learn to view breakdowns as valuable learning opportunities. When an individual or team understands why they failed to deliver on a promise, they can use that insight to bolster future performance.

Formally Declaring a Breakdown

Having an explicit conversation about missed targets or broken agreements gives people an opportunity to address the issue, learn from the experience, and invest into the ongoing working relationship. This puts the issue on the radar and addresses it proactively—an empowering move. When things are considered to be working, the habit tends to be business as usual. When someone demonstrates the courage to declare a breakdown, people are snapped out of their ordinary habits and can mobilize and act in new ways.

Working With Breakdowns

First, you need to actually declare the breakdown.

This means you need to call it to the attention of the person who made the commitment and discuss it. Allow people the time and space to express how they feel about the breakdown and, if necessary, vent their emotions. Take inventory of the situation while separating objective facts from subjective interpretations. It is important to acknowledge honestly and objectively what happened or didn't happen.

What percentage of the goal (or milestone) was achieved?

What was the impact (in terms of people, relationships, energy, costs, etc.)?

Learn from the breakdown by asking, "How did this happen?" This is not an occasion for blame or excuses, but rather an objective analysis of the circumstances that led to or created the breakdown.

Did another unanticipated priority take precedence over this one?

Was the original goal unrealistic?

Was the scope of the objective broader than the resources available?

Was time mismanaged?

Was coordination or communication a factor?

Were there circumstances outside our control?

Then, make a renewed commitment.

If the failure to deliver on the commitment creates a cost to the person who originally made the request in terms of time, inconvenience, pressure, etc., then it is essential to discuss these costs as part of the conversation to correct the breakdown, and make good on the original or revised promise.

What is the intention going forward? What are the specific actions required?

What are the new conditions for satisfaction?

Are there requests from others that will need to be made?

If necessary, adjust any relevant work structuring documents.

Example: Create a modified action plan with updated milestones.

As a manager, when you hone the skills in this book, you can significantly expand your ability to add value to your organization. Beyond simply being a tool to help individuals and teams execute more effectively, over time, the practice of accountability cultivates a culture of accountability.

DECISION MAKING

What do managers actually do?
Well, they make plans, support people and processes, make decisions and communicate to implement those decisions.

Of all of these activities of managers, one of the most misunderstood and poorly executed is decision-making.

The way an organization makes decisions can often be a huge source of stress, frustration, difficulty, conflict, and, ultimately failure.

As discussed in other sections of this book, especially the section on *Responsibility and Authority,* for organizations to reach high performance, they must have clear lines of responsibility and authority.

While some organizations do have detailed job descriptions that outline each roles' and responsibilities, few organizations have detailed out the explicit authority of each role.

One of the most useful ways that organizations can tease out the explicit authority that each role has to allocate resources (bandwidth and budget) is to itemize all of the decisions that must be made each week, month, quarter and year.

By making decisions explicit, it removes the ambiguity and confusion that often puzzle and frustrate many managers and teams.

Upon initial reflection, this seems simple enough. Just list all the decisions and who has the authority to make them. And yes, this represents a huge step forward for most organizations and removes countless obstacles and frustrations so that the teams can more easily move forward toward their goals.

However, there is more to decision-making than just listing them and indicating who makes the decision. There is actually a lot of nuances around making decisions.

In this section, we will introduce a few best practices and a specific tool called the Decision Matrix that you can use to significantly enhance your organizational effectiveness.

Consider how many decisions each manager in your company makes each week. Now multiply that estimated figure by approximately fifty weeks in a year. Now multiply that figure by the number of managers in your company.

It's a big number!

The Institute for Employment Studies in the United Kingdom has performed a lot of research on decision-making and how it impacts employees in that country. Their research suggests that decision-making is the basis of approximately 50% of employee engagement.

This means that the quality of the decisions you and the other managers in your company make represents about half of what determines your level of employee engagement.

The well-known and well-researched consulting firm, Bain, estimates that decision-making effectiveness is 95% correlated with financial performance.

Bain's research suggests that the quality of your decisions has a 95% correlation to how successful your company will be in financial terms.

Yet, most managers in typical companies have had little to no training in the art and science of decision-making. Even more troubling, most managers and departments have not even articulated the key decisions and put them in writing.

A number of studies have highlighted the quality of decision-making in many companies as being nothing short of dismal. In some studies, the vast majority of decisions made are considered to be ineffective or inadequate.

If decision practices are so important, why is so little attention put on them?

There are many factors contributing to this, including under-funded and under-staffed departments, demanding workloads that often allow just enough bandwidth to keep up with the volume of work, and the fact that many managers and leaders haven't had the benefit of training programs like this one.

The good news is that you and the other leaders and managers in your organization are getting the training and tools you need to seriously elevate your decision making.

Like all management skills and methods, there are best practices, hundreds of books and thousands of articles and countless training programs available. The issue is that most managers are just too busy to dig through the large volume of information.

Another good thing is that you don't need to go through and read dozens of books or take in-depth courses on every management skill. The most important thing is to be educated on the basic best practices that research shows work in most situations pretty well.

Just being familiar with the best practices and having a few tools in your toolkit to practice with can work wonders, as you have probably already seen in this leadership program.

Some studies have shown that when managers take into account and use some of the widely available best practices and tools, they are able to exceed expectations by more than double, cut failure rates in half, and significantly increase the number of good decisions by as much as four or five-fold.

It is beyond the scope of this short section to delineate the nuance of the art and science of decision-making. There are many excellent books that do this. For our purposes here, we will summarize a few of the most useful best practices that are likely to pay large dividends for you and most of the managers in your organization.

List the Strategic Drivers that are Relevant to this Decision

Strategic drivers were introduced in the section of this book entitled "Strategic Thinking Primer." In that section, we highlighted the necessity to identify the "driving forces" inherent in the situation or context

These strategic drivers are the forces that are impacting the situation and calling for a decision to be made.

According to Clayton Christensen, defining the issue correctly is the first and most important action in any problem-solving process, including strategic thinking or decision-making.

Most management teams do not, as a whole, understand the real issues underlying the threats and opportunities they face.

A fundamental cause of a lack of alignment, for many management teams, is a lack of understanding.

The business world's graveyards are filled with organizations whose executives implemented elegant answers to the wrong questions.

So clearly, the "driving forces" must be named and articulated clearly so that the decisions that are made are answers to the right questions (or solutions to the right issues).

Do a Stakeholder Analysis

It would be difficult to consider a decision to be a good one if it failed to take into account the people (or groups) that would be impacted by it. Therefore, it is crucial to do a stakeholder analysis and list all of the people and groups that have a stake in this decision.

Consider the Business Impact of the Decision

Before making any significant decision, brainstorm 3-5 business goals or outcomes that may be impacted (positively or negatively) by the proposed decision.

While it is useful for you to do this alone, it is more effective to brainstorm this question with several of the stakeholders who have knowledge of this area of the business and/or may be impacted directly or indirectly by the decision.

(It would be a great idea to include all of the key stakeholders identified during the stakeholder analysis).

Consider Your Alternatives Carefully

How can you know if you are making a good decision if you are not aware of your alternatives?

In business, more options usually lead to better decisions.

Take the necessary time to determine what options and alternatives are available and do at least a little bit of analysis on these options before narrowing them down to the ones you are deciding on.

We recommend exercising the discipline of writing down at least three viable alternatives before making a decision on one of them.

Put the Decision in Writing and Indicate Everyone Who Participated

Decisions that are not in writing, not documented with some kind of paper trail can be called "Phantom Decisions". Phantoms are elusive and can pose any number of problems. Every time a critical decision is made, write down exactly what was decided, why that decision was made, and who was involved in the process. Articulate this in an email or message to the key stakeholders to establish a paper trail for future reference.

Now that we have reviewed a few of the most applicable best practices for decision-making in general, we can turn our attention to the specific decisions that you make in your functional area each week, month, quarter and year.

This is no longer an academic exercise. We are going to begin to work with the actual decisions that are impacting your organization right now, this month and every month going forward.

When you implement the framework we are about to introduce to you, you will be able to expect to accelerate your business results while decreasing the stress, frustration, tension and conflict that many departments and functional areas struggle with.

Making Your Decisions Explicit

Reflect for a moment on all the decisions that are made by your team or department, about how to allocate resources, including people's time and focus, as well as the company's assets and capital.

Consider…
Hiring decisions.
Budget decisions.
Job titles and job descriptions.
Scheduling.
Process steps and sequences. Policy changes.

Now, make a list of 10-15 decisions that you or your team (or peers) make to keep your operation running smoothly each week, each month, each quarter and each year.

Three Types of Decisions

Now that you are warmed up and are thinking about decision-making, consider decisions in your department or functional area that fall into three specific categories.

The first category is decisions that you are authorized to make each week, each month and each quarter (that you do not need your boss' approval).

Write down as many decisions that you can think of that you are authorized to make (without anyone else's approval).

The second category is decisions that you make that are subject to your boss' approval (that she or he might veto).

The third category is decisions that are made by other people on your team or in your department whom you have invited to provide input. This includes decisions that you don't make on your own but that you can make recommendations about.

It also includes the many issues that you are consulted on before a decision is made because either you may be asked to help implement the decision or your work might be impacted by the decision.

Now that you have done this exercise, download the Decision Matrix worksheet below and fill it out either on your own, or better, with your team.

Name of Decision	Input	Decide	Approve

You will see that the matrix has three columns that correspond to the three categories of decisions you brainstormed above: those you can make without approval, those that require your boss' approval, and those for which you have been asked for input.

During the above brainstorming exercise, we emphasized you as the person giving input or making the decision. But for purposes of the matrix for your team or department, you will also include the names and or titles of many other stakeholders into the matrix.

There are three roles associated with decision-making. People who give input, people who decide, and people who approve (or VETO) those decisions.

Input

These people are often required to have buy-in for successful implementation of final decisions. They must have visibility during the decision process and are generally required to comment on the decision.

Decide

This is the person (usually one individual) who owns the decision process and is the one ultimately accountable for the results of the decision. The decision is still subject to being overridden by their boss who must give final approval (and sign off on the decision).

Approve

This person may or may not have full visibility into the details of the decision process up to this point but is required to sign off on the decision (with veto power) as a part of the organization's checks and balances. This is usually the person the decision-maker reports to. You may recall that we identified this person as "your boss" in the above paragraph.

Now you have it!

All the tools you need to significantly elevate the quality of your decision-making while also eliminating confusion and frustration in your department.

The next step is to review this information with your team (and / or key stakeholders) and schedule a meeting, or multiple meetings, to complete your Decision Matrix as a group so that all involved understand exactly what decisions were made in your organization and the precise process with which they were made.

This concludes our discussion of the skill set of "Performance Management. Now we move on to the next skill set, "Project Implementation."

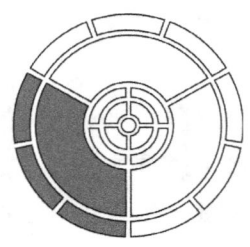

CHAPTER 7: IMPLEMENTATION

First, I define this skill set as follows. "Project Implementation is concerned with planning quarterly and monthly projects, defining objectives, workstreams, tasks, and timelines, and coordinating all of the people and activities necessary to stay on track with milestones and budget until successful completion."

Team Discussion

When you initiate a conversation with your employees and team(s), you could use some version of the following questions.

- How do we currently plan our quarterly and monthly projects?

- How do we define objectives, workstreams, tasks and timelines?

- How do we currently coordinate the people and activities necessary to stay on track with project milestones and budgets?

Benchmarks

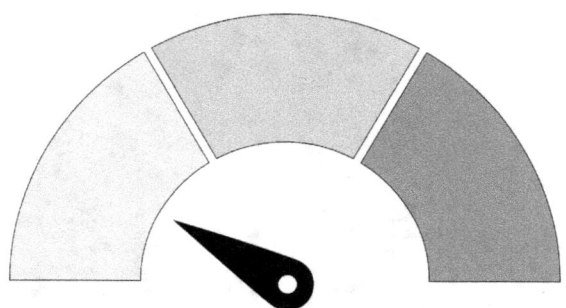

IMPLEMENTATION LOWER RANGE

A leader and a team functioning in the lower range of proficiency in this skill set might describe it this way.

My team is not using any kind of formal project management methodology. We use informal methods to plan projects and manage them, and we use simple tools such as spreadsheets and written documents (we don't use shared dashboards or project management software).

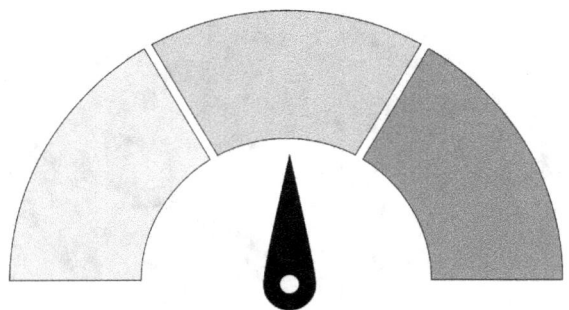

IMPLEMENTATION MIDDLE RANGE

A leader and a team functioning in the middle range of proficiency in this skill set might describe it this way.

I have some training in project management and some of my team members use project management tools, however, this is inconsistent, and could use improvement. Some projects are run tightly, while others are managed loosely. It is still common to have milestones and deadlines missed.

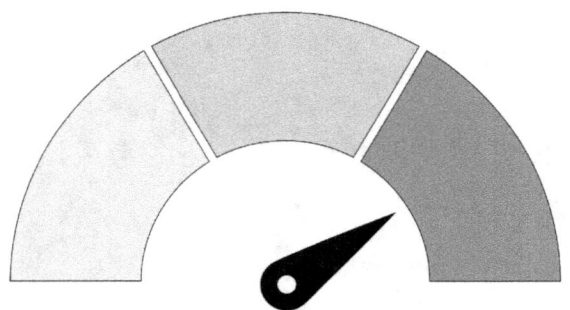

IMPLEMENTATION HIGHER RANGE

A leader and a team functioning in the higher range of proficiency in this skill set might describe it this way.

We use sophisticated project management methods and tools to plan projects carefully, to clarify the work streams, and to manage milestones, tasks and deadlines. We have a shared dashboard in our project management system so that everyone knows the progress toward each milestone.

Connecting Strategic Planning and Project Management

Clarifying organizational priorities and developing strategic plans (for example, annual plans and quarterly plans) were discussed in the chapter on Dynamic Steering. There must be a strong linkage between those annual and quarterly plans and the numerous efforts, undertakings, work streams or as we prefer to call them, "Projects."

Some organizations develop strong strategic plans, and some organizations do a good job at managing projects. However, for an organization to be able to execute its plans, they have to link strategic planning with project management.

In many, if not most cases, the people creating the plans are different from the people executing those plans! And too often, the strategic plans are disconnected from any kind of project implementation.

This is a long-standing challenge in many organizations.

However, in my book in this *Integral Leadership* series entitled *Strategy & Alignment,* I introduce a tool called the *Prioritization Matrix* as a primary method to help you develop your annual and quarterly strategic plans. A "prioritization matrix" uses "Effort / Cost" is on the vertical axis and "Value / Impact" is on the horizontal. It is a way to map out the projects (also the opportunities and issues) a leader or team recognizes and organizing them from "least leverage" to "most leverage".

In my 25 years coaching and advising leaders and leadership teams, I have found that one of the most important "practices" is what I call "Prioritizing According to Leverage."

Here is a simple illustration of what this kind of matrix will look like:

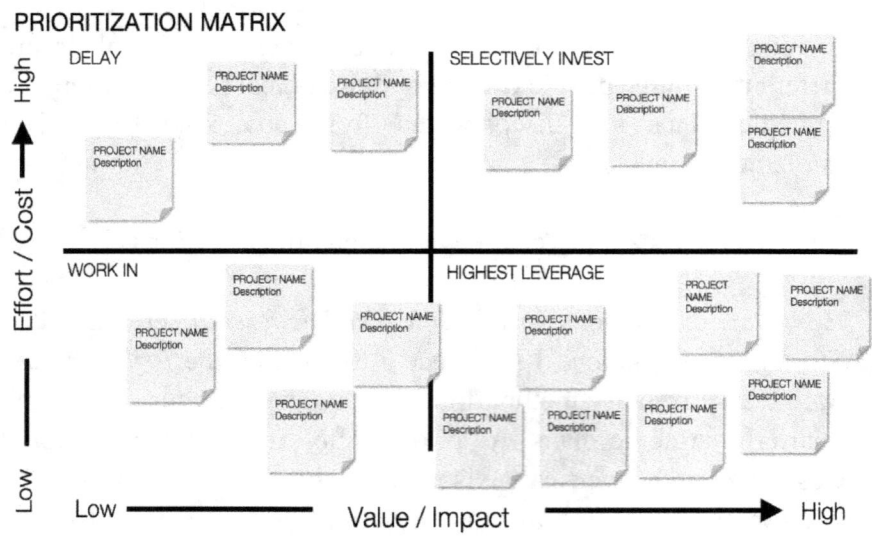

Take a look at this example of a Prioritization Matrix with various projects distributed across the four sections. The large initiatives that you will work on this year are in the upper right quadrant labeled "Selectively Invest, " reflecting the fact that they are not just high impact but also high effort.

Also note the "Delay" and "Work In" quadrants reflecting low impact, high effort, and low impact, low effort respectively.

Your highest-leverage priorities for each calendar quarter are represented in
the lower-right labeled "Highest Leverage," reflecting the fact that these efforts are high impact but the relatively low effort (compared to your other priorities this year).

The key to connecting strategic planning with project management is to make sure that every single one of your priorities on your Prioritization Matrix (signified in this illustration by Post-It notes) has a separate Project Plan that answers the five project planning questions.

While it may sound deceptively simple, this is the key.

If you have priorities in your strategic plan (represented by the projects on your matrix) that do not have a written Project Plan that answers the five questions (Why, What, How, When and Who) then your strategic planning is not linked with your project management.

This means that the likelihood of your strategic plan being successfully executed is extremely low. Clearly, this has an implication for your credibility as a manager and a leader.

To make sure that your organization executes on its strategic plan, make sure that every priority has a written project plan.

Your Prioritization Matrix should be reviewed frequently. Ideally, this happens weekly in your weekly planning. And you should be updating these monthly to stay current as circumstances in your business environment continually shift.

Similarly, Project Plans should be updated weekly or bi-weekly as tasks are completed, milestones are met or adjusted, and work streams are implemented. You will update your project plans every time your project teams meet.

Ideally, the Task List portion of your project plan (the When? And the Who? elements) should live in a shared dashboard in your Project Management Platform so that all project team members and stakeholders can view the shared task list (dashboard) to update progress on tasks.

Once your strategic plans are fully linked to your project planning systems, then your organizational capacity for what is widely known as "execution" will take a giant leap forward.

You can expect that your annual and quarterly objectives will be met with much higher levels of consistency. As you and your team increase your/their skill in using these tools, the organizational capacity for execution will continue to expand quarter by quarter.

The result of this increase in execution capacity will be that your team or department will be able to set more ambitious goals each year with high levels of confidence that you will hit those targets.

Fundamentals of Project Management

A simple definition of "project" is an "effort" that managers and teams undertake with a specific definition of success (or deliverables), usually combined with a clear beginning and end to that effort.

Projects are distinct from the ongoing management activities that might be called "management responsibilities" or "operations". Roughly half of the work managers undertake in the workplace would fall into this second category of ongoing responsibilities. We might think of these as well-defined processes, routines, or weekly activities. In other words, "operations". The other half of activities that managers are usually engaged in are the efforts that we will call "projects". Quality management pioneer Joseph Juran defines a project as "a problem scheduled for a solution". While this definition may be technically correct, the word "problem" does not fully capture the opportunities that are, in fact, the motivation behind many projects.

A project may be undertaken to capitalize on a business opportunity, or to improve a process that will enable greater success for the organization.

For example, a project could be started to design and implement an employee training program, to design a new product or upgrade an existing product, or to restructure a department. In addition to thoughtfully planning a project, to achieve the intended outcome, projects must be actively managed in specific ways over time, from inception to completion.

Before beginning a project, it is important to take time to determine the problem the project is trying to solve or the opportunity it is attempting to capitalize on.

Popular project management author and expert James P. Lewis once wrote, "Projects do not fail at the end; they fail at the beginning". While some projects are more simple and others are more complex, every project plan should offer the stakeholders' clarity on the answers to five fundamental questions. For simplicity's sake, we will frame these project planning questions as... Why? What? How? When? Who? We will look at each of these project planning questions in more detail in a separate training video.

Clearly, good intentions are never enough to implement a project successfully. The details of the activities and tasks associated with the project, must be managed carefully. And this especially includes the human element of every project: the people doing the work. In another section, we will review the keys to managing project activities over time so that your projects will be concluded successfully with the best chance of achieving their stated purposes and goals.

Project Planning

Many managers are self-described "action takers" and "doers". These managers enjoy getting things done, accomplishing outcomes, and making progress. Perhaps you can identify with this?

While this is certainly a positive thing, the downside is that many managers have a bias for "doing" over "planning". Experience shows that most projects that fail, suffer more from poor planning than poor implementation.

Unfortunately, many managers' performance suffers, along with their departments and even their broader organization's, as a result of "successfully implementing a poorly designed strategy". The old, familiar saying is perhaps cliche and an oversimplification, but it is nevertheless relevant here. "If you fail to plan, you plan to fail".

One well-known project management expert has estimated that each hour allotted to project planning results in a three-hour decrease in the time it takes to successfully implement the project. It is also worth highlighting that well-planned projects are far more likely to result in success than poorly-planned projects. As the other, familiar saying goes, "An ounce of prevention is equal to a pound of cure". Clearly, not all projects are the same. Complex projects require a comprehensive, detailed project plan.

Other projects are more modest in scope and may be implemented with a basic "action plan" that primarily consists of a task list. Yet, even small projects require clarity on the reason for the project, the intended outcomes (or deliverables), and some indication of who is going to do what tasks (and when).

Keep in mind that while a detailed project plan may be essential in the early phases of a large, complex project, the act of planning is not necessarily a one-time event that takes place only at the start.

For large projects, it may take several iterations of the plan before the kick-off. It may also require ongoing updating of the plan as new information becomes available (including the results from the initial stages of the project efforts). This is sometimes referred to as "dynamic steering".

A project plan should answer five questions, which we summarize as... Why, what, how, when, and who?

Why

"Why" refers to the purpose of the project. Put another way, the reason for undertaking the effort.

The purpose of the project must take into account the context of the department, the organization and its needs and opportunities in the current time frame. The time frame could be this year, this quarter or even this month, and should be informed by internal and external organizational circumstances.

What

"What" refers to the outcomes or deliverables of the project. Put another way, this is what the organization will have in place after the project concludes successfully. You can think of the "what" as the objectives of the project.

Note that "what" is not the specific actions, work streams or tasks. Nor is it the "milestones" of the project. Those are covered under another section of the project plan. Think of the "what" as "What will we have when the project is completed successfully".

How

The "how" refers to the way the project will be pursued. The "approach" or the "strategy" behind the project. The "how" refers to the methods, the "work streams" and the "sub-projects" that must be undertaken in order for the whole project to succeed. Think of this as "How we will succeed with this project".

When answering this question, you will need to brainstorm the relevant details of the project so that no important consideration is overlooked.

Some managers think of this as "framing" out the work to be done into major issues and activities, along with a breakdown of each. This results in a high-level action plan that outlines major activities, responsibilities and the basic timeline.

When And Who

The "when" and "who" questions are answered by what we can refer to as a "Task List". Each major work stream, or sub-project, should have its own task list.

You are already familiar with a task list. It essentially lists the name of the task, the target completion date (when), and the person responsible for completing the task by the date (who). Every project should have a project plan. The five project planning questions (Why, What, How, When, Who) can be answered briefly, or thoroughly, depending on the complexity of the project., we will put this Project Plan to good use as we look at managing an active project to successful completion.

Managing an Active Project

The implementation of a successful project comes down to actually doing the "how" (the work streams) that have been outlined in the project plan. With an emphasis on the exact tasks that are detailed in the "when" and the "who" sections of the project plan. There are two different ways to view the "when" and "who" of a project plan.

1. The task lists associated with each work stream (or sub-project).

2. The major milestones and due dates of key tasks seen on the project schedule, timeline or "Gantt Chart".

Different organizations, teams and managers use different tools to manage their "Tasks Lists". While some managers use a spreadsheet to track their specific tasks, with target dates and the person responsible for each. Many organizations prefer the efficiency and visibility that formal project management software tools provide.

Tasks lists detail every single task, grouped according to work streams and deliverable milestones. These lists should include a clear description of the task, the name of the person responsible for it, the target completion date, and optionally, the current percentage completed.

The Project Schedule (milestone calendar or Gantt Chart) indicates the major milestones or deliverables which are outcomes as a result of the completion of groups of tasks. The project schedule details the timeline and sequence of the major steps that must be completed for the project to be successful.

This is especially important for complex projects with multiple work streams and teams whose work needs to be well-coordinated. Ultimately, the best way to keep a project on track is for each team member to assume responsibility for his or her own work. The essence of managing a project to completion is to have regularly scheduled project team meetings.

Depending on the scope and timeline of a project, this could be bi-weekly, weekly, or even daily.

During these project team meetings, the project plan, task list, and project schedule are reviewed together with the team. Any deviation from the plan is discussed, and the team members can collaborate to resolve scheduling conflicts or support bottlenecks or sticking points as the project unfolds.

The following conditions make it much easier for a project leader to keep his or her project on track.

1. Clearly defined tasks that tie back to the project plan (the work streams).

2. Each person responsible for each task has the knowledge and skills necessary to complete it successfully.

3. Each person must manage his/her time effectively so that enough time is scheduled on his/her calendar each week to complete the tasks by the deadline.

4. Team members provide updates about progress, including receiving feedback and input on best ways to coordinate work and complete the tasks correctly.

5. A clear definition of scope of project and authority to take corrective action if the project gets off track or is no longer on the intended timeline.

Delegation

Delegation is a skill that does not come naturally to many managers and leaders. In this section, we will outline several techniques that can help you level up your delegation skills.

Before we describe six specific "best practices" for delegation, we need to first address a mindset problem. The problem is that many leaders and managers adopt an "individual contributor" mindset rather than a "manager" or "executive" mindset.

If you adopt the individual contributor mindset, no amount of best practices will help you get good at delegation because that mindset is fundamentally ill-suited for delegation. When you move from an individual contributor role to a manager role, your job fundamentally changes.

Individual contributors use their specific knowledge and skills to add value through their time and effort. Conversely, a manager's responsibility is to "manage".

As a manager, you will of course add some value through your own efforts. However, most of the work of a manager is to support and guide processes, people and activities toward specific outcomes or targets.

Put simply, the vast majority of the value a manager brings is in supporting and guiding the efforts of the team or group (and the processes associated with the department or function).

When you adopt a manager's mindset, you recognize that your value is in supporting and guiding people and processes to achieve shared goals (outcomes and targets) over time.

When you maintain a manager's mindset, you recognize that your success is represented by the team, group or department's success. As a manager, yes you are on the team, but your main role is "team captain" whose primary responsibility is to help the team succeed.

When you maintain a manager's mindset, you realize that you are responsible for helping your team members succeed. This means supporting them and guiding them to increase their knowledge and skill, and their ability to perform their job well.

When you maintain a manager's mindset, you are quick to give credit to other team members to bolster their confidence and slow to take credit for yourself. Your credit comes when your team, group or department hits its monthly and quarterly milestones.

Now that you are committed to cultivating and strengthening your manager's mindset, the following six delegation best practices will help you rapidly elevate your delegation ability.

1. Distinguish Between Types of Tasks

It will be very helpful for you to make a key distinction between three different kinds of tasks as it relates to delegation of work and assignments to the men and women who report to you.

The first category of work, or tasks, are those that only you can do. There are some things that only you can do.

Perhaps no one else on your team has the knowledge and skills required to complete that task. And the amount of education or training (perhaps months or years) is impractical given the nature of the work and the timeline it is expected to be completed in.

The second category of work, or tasks, are those that others can do with some guidance.

This is the category of work that does require some explanation and may require ongoing check-ins, feedback, iteration or other kinds of support as the assignment progresses.

The third category of work, or tasks, are those that others can do with no guidance.

Clearly, there are many tasks that fall well within the existing abilities of the people on your team.

Every team member is hired with certain innate abilities and those abilities grow with experience.

If you are effective in your role as manager and leader, the ability of the men and women who report to you should grow over time as you train, guide and support them.

It takes little effort to delegate tasks in this third category with confidence that the team member will complete them successfully.

With some effort, you can delegate tasks in the second category.

This is why you have communication systems and regular team meetings to allow the time and space to provide the necessary guidance your people need to complete the work in this category.

This brings us to the first category we listed, the work that only you can do.

Our rule of thumb is this – You should primarily do the work that only you can do.

If you are doing work in the second and third categories, in a certain sense you are doing other people's jobs.

When you spend time doing other people's jobs, it leaves little time to do your own.

And clearly, there is plenty of work to be done in the first category, the work that only you can do.

2. Leverage Accountability Conversations

Some managers dash off an email or a text message to an employee or team member with a task they want to be done.

But if the recipient of that "request" does not agree to do it, then in a very real sense, the task was not actually delegated, it was merely suggested.

As a manager who is serious about becoming more effective at delegation, stop suggesting tasks and start delegating tasks.

The difference between suggesting a task vs. delegating a task is the validation from the other person that they understood the assignment and that they can, in fact, complete it as requested by the deadline.

We call this an "accountability conversation". It may be as short as an email reply or a quick discussion, but the expectation must be made explicit and the other people must confirm that they will do it according to instructions by the date requested.

When you delegate assignments (or ask someone to complete a task), you should establish what we call "clear conditions for satisfaction".

Put another way, you must make it absolutely clear what you need and the criteria for success with the assignment or task.

One of the most important aspects of what we call an "Effective Request" is the due date of the task.

If you attempt to delegate a task but fail to let the other person know when you need it done, then it could be said that you only suggested a task, and have not actually formally delegated it.

Unless the people you are delegating to accept the assignment by offering clear "committed responses" and confirm that they understand the expectations and are committing to complete the task by the given date, then it has not really been effectively delegated.

If there is no validation of the request and a "committed response", then you have not thoroughly delegated the task. In a certain sense, you have really just made a request of an employee.

If they don't clarify the expectation and agree to the terms, then it is hard to feel confident that they will meet the expectation.

3. Delegate According to Current Ability

If you consider the three categories of work described previously, the second and third categories contain tasks that others can perform successfully either with no guidance or with some guidance and support.

Clearly, this is a function of a person's ability.

If you are unclear about what your team members are capable of then you have some homework to do before you can be an effective manager and leader.

Employees are hired, in part, due to their qualifications. This is another word for ability.

Employees also undertake company onboarding and training to increase the abilities they will need to be successful in their roles.

As a manager, you must know what your team members are capable of. If you have done your homework, it should be relatively easy to know if a person is capable of a given task.

If you don't know or aren't sure if they are capable, there is a simple and effective method to find out.

Ask them.

Part of delegation is to have a conversation with the person you want to delegate the task to.

Ask them if they understand the assignment. Ask them how confident they are that it can be completed successfully (on time) easily. Check in with them.

If they hesitate or demonstrate anxiety or confusion about the assignment, then this tells you everything you need to know.

It's your job to offer guidance and support your employees' needs to be successful in their jobs. And, in some cases, it's your job to replace the team member with someone who does have the requisite capabilities.

4. Delegate to Increase Ability

Part of your responsibility as a manager and leader is to increase your team's (or functional areas') capability over time.

Recalling the three categories of work, the second category, tasks that employees can complete with some guidance and support, is crucial to giving your employees opportunities to learn, increase their confidence, make small recoverable mistakes and grow in the process.

If you aren't delegating tasks that give the men and women who report to you an opportunity to learn, then you are missing an important opportunity.

As a leader, you should take some calculated risks. Effective managers know mistakes will occasionally be made, balls will occasionally be dropped, and deadlines will sometimes be missed. This is a crucial part of the learning process and is absolutely necessary for effective teamwork.

As an effective manager, over time, you get to know your employees' and teammates' unique strengths and weaknesses.

Some people are self-starters and require little supervision. Others require a little more input, feedback, guidance, support, encouragement and reassurance, especially as you support your employees in their category 2 assignments.

As a manager, you have certain constraints you must operate your area under.

This includes limitations on budget and bandwidth. It is much easier to help an existing team member expand their skills than to obtain a larger labor budget to hire additional people who have the needed skills.

So effective delegation includes both delegating tasks according to current ability and delegating tasks to increase ability.

5. Always Give Clear Instructions

Managers who are effective at delegation take the necessary time, usually a few seconds or a minute or two, to articulate the assignment or task clearly, and provide the information needed to complete the task.

Effective delegation is never ambiguous, confusing, or frustrating.

It is both inconsiderate and a reflection of poor management skills to delegate assignments to employees without the benefit of clear, helpful instruction. Effective managers are seen by their employees as professional and considerate.

When you delegate a task, include all necessary information, indicate where exactly to find any additional information needed to complete the task, and tell them where to go for support if they get stuck or hit a roadblock.

Even if the task seems obvious to you, make sure to include specific, clear, and detailed instructions.

Do not assume that your teammate has all the same information that you have, or recalls all the details of the work that you do. That is neither professional nor considerate. Bear in mind the experience of the other person on the other side of your delegation.

If you are perceived to be thoughtful, professional, friendly and helpful when you delegate, then that will have a huge implication on your teamwork and your credibility as a manager and a leader.

On the other hand, if you delegate a task to a team member and they perceive you as being short, terse, impatient, entitled, or unappreciative, it can have implications for your teamwork and how you are perceived as a leader.

If you have specific preferences for how the assignment will be carried out, make sure to include those details. If you have a strict deadline or under tight pressure, or there are specific milestones that must be hit, be perfectly clear about all of that.

Ask yourself, "Am I setting this person up for success?"

Including all pertinent details and clear instructions from the start will circumvent many delays and misunderstandings that can impact the success of the project.

6. Trust But Verify

This best practice speaks to the balance you must strike between, on the one hand, giving the person the benefit of the doubt (and showing respect for his/her ability). On the other hand, following up to make sure nothing has been missed, or overlooked, or if more guidance is needed to ensure success.

Always be proactive with your communication, including following up after a task is delegated.

You do not want to be perceived as a micro-manager who is watching too closely over your employee's shoulder.

You want to give your teammates some leeway to tackle the work the way he or she feels is best. However, it is necessary to occasionally step in and verify that the task is moving along as needed and planned.

For example, if you delegated tasks a week ago that are due tomorrow, trust that your employees are on top of things... but send quick verification messages to check-in, ask if they are on track or if they need any support in case any snags are hit.

Following up in this way cultivates trust and respect within your team. You are showing faith in their ability, but also sending a clear message that this is a team effort and you are available for support.

You should do occasional "check-ins" to make sure the other person understands the key elements of the assignment as you intend it.

Missed deadlines and slipping milestones are to be expected. No one has a 100% performance score over time. Misunderstandings occur. Life happens.

When you put these guidelines into practice, over time, your delegation skills will increase along with the quality of your communication and teamwork.

It can be helpful to remember, relationships take time to develop. And, feedback is crucial if you are going to enhance the level of trust you have with the people who report to you. Take the time to discuss the working relationship and how the delegation process is going.

In this section, you have learned a number of critical techniques that will help you strengthen your delegation skills.

Try to focus primarily on the work that only you can do, and try to delegate much of the rest. Bear in mind the current ability of the people you are delegating to and use stretch assignments to help expand your abilities.

Be rigorous with the instructions you give when you delegate using accountability conversations. In time, you and your team will develop greater trust and excel at this crucial activity.

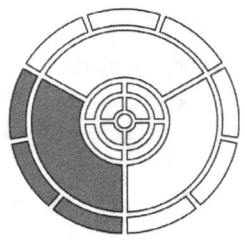

CHAPTER 8: PRODUCTIVITY

First we begin our discussion of this skill set with a clear definition and the benchmarks for levels of proficiency in this area. I define this skill set by saying, "Improving Productivity is concerned with your ability to help your organization complete work in a productive, organized, efficient and effective way, including managing calendars and tasks, running effective meetings, and staying focused and proactive in the face of distractions, urgencies, and obstacles."

Team Discussion

When you initiate a conversation with your employees and team(s), you could use some version of the following questions.

- How do we help our team members complete work in a productive, organized, efficient and effective way?

- How do we (and our team) currently manage calendars and tasks?

- How do we approach meetings?

- How do we keep people focused and proactive in the face of distractions and obstacles?

Benchmarks

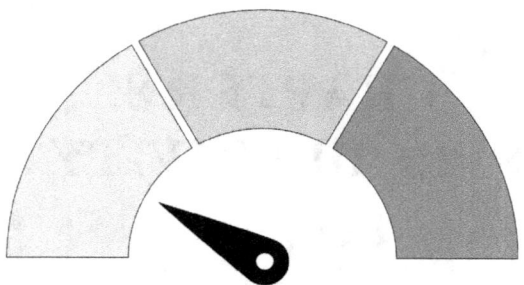

PRODUCTIVITY LOWER RANGE

A leader and a team functioning in the lower range of proficiency in this skill set might describe it this way.

We are hard workers but we have not had the benefit of tools or training in time management / task management. Some team members are naturally focused, but many are easily distracted and often inefficient with their time. The complaints that our meetings are inefficient are pretty accurate.

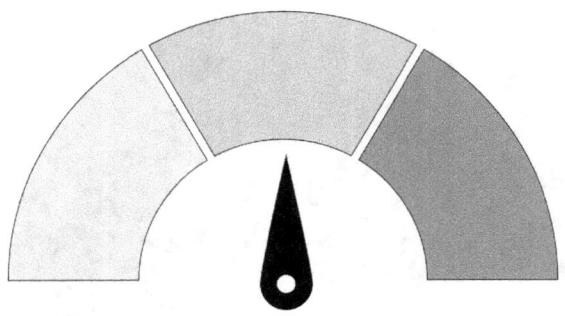

PRODUCTIVITY MIDDLE RANGE

A leader and a team functioning in the middle range of proficiency in this skill set might describe it this way.

Our productivity is spotty. Some team members are very focused and efficient, and others simply lack good time management habits. Some weeks we are focused and proactive, but at other times we are firefighting or getting distracted.

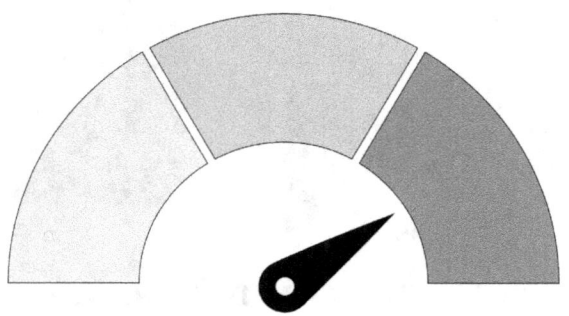

PRODUCTIVITY HIGHER RANGE

A leader and a team functioning in the higher range of proficiency in this skill set might describe it this way.

We consistently enjoy high levels of productivity. We are well-trained in productivity best practices and tools, are highly organized, and use our calendars and task management systems effectively. We keep distractions to a minimum and protect our ability to focus and stay proactive.

ATTENTION MANAGEMENT

Conventional thinking suggests that managing time is the key to higher productivity. Time management techniques were most useful in an era when employees punched a time clock, came to a factory at set hours, and performed similar work daily on an assembly line or desk. But in many organizations today, work is done more with the mind than with the hands, and as much on a mobile device in the cloud or while on the go as at a desk in an office. When the value of work is in relationships, ideas, decisions, and outcomes, more than being at a certain place for a certain amount of time, the time management paradigm starts to break down.

Time management alone is inadequate in an always-on, continually connected workplace riddled with portable computers, smart phones, tablets, never-ending email, and ever-increasing apps that are all vying for our attention.

Concentration is like a muscle. And many workers have literally lost their ability to focus and concentrate as a result of not using that muscle. In the worst case, managers ricochet from one urgent task to the next, unable to bring their full concentration to any one activity for more than a few minutes at a time.

You may know people like this. They spend virtually every waking hour being "busy", putting out fires, and racing from task to task, and leave little time for planning, reflection, preventative maintenance or renewal.

Misinformed, thinking that multitasking is actually a good thing, they stumble around in a fog of "continuous partial attention".

In a conference call, they miss key information because they are simultaneously typing an email. At lunch, they are constantly glancing at their phones, missing the nuance of what their coworker is explaining, or worse, rudely answering a call as the person right in front of them is in mid-sentence.

This is problematic enough when line-level employees are distracted and unfocused.

When managers and leaders indulge in these behaviors and fail to bring their full attention and, therefore, intelligence to their responsibilities, their performance and the performance of their department or division suffer.

Webster's Dictionary defines attention as... The act or state of attending or heeding; the application of the mind to any sensible object, representation, or thought. Focused awareness. Observant consideration; to notice. Close or careful observing or listening. Webster's Thesaurus lists the following synonyms for attention: observation, regard, notice, mindfulness, listening, concentration, care, consideration, heedfulness, alertness, attentiveness, intentness, thoroughness, and awareness.

In times past, working with attention was something left to professional athletes, elite soldiers, martial artists, and yoga and meditation practitioners.

But due to the advances and proliferation of digital technology and media, which constantly demand workers' attention, business leaders now recognize that attention, like other finite resources, must be managed.

Thomas Davenport and John Beck were pioneers in the field of attention management. In their groundbreaking book, The Attention Economy, they make a strong case that, "understanding and managing attention is now the single most important determinant of business success". Davenport and Beck introduced the term "organizational ADD" (attention deficit disorder) to bring awareness to some aspects of the ineffective working style described above. They write, "Today's businesses are heading for disaster unless they can overcome the dangerously high attention deficits that threaten to cripple today's workplace".

They define organizational ADD as an "increased likelihood of missing key information when making decisions, diminished time for reflection on anything, but simple informational transactions, difficulty holding others' attention, and decreased ability to focus when necessary". This management training offers specific frameworks and practices managers can use to boost productivity, reduce reactive behavior (and the stress that goes along with it), and allocate more time and energy to the activities that matter most. In this training we will be exploring what it means to bring more awareness to our day-to-day and week-to-week management activities.

Bringing more awareness and more discipline to where you place your attention and how you manage that focus, in your role as manager, can help you reduce the reactive "fire fighting" that characterizes many manager's work experiences. "Companies that succeed in the future will be those experts not in time management, but in attention management".

> *"Understanding and managing attention is now the single most important determinant of business success."*
> *– Thomas Davenport and John Beck, authors of the book The Attention Economy.*

Too many managers confuse efficiency with effectiveness. Efficiency is doing more things in less time. Effectiveness is doing the most important things well. While efficiency is doing "more things," effectiveness can be thought of as "doing the right things."'

To paraphrase the late Stephen Covey, author of the bestsellers, *The 7 Habits of Highly Effective People* and First Things First... Efficiency is a jet airplane traveling at 600 miles per hour.

Effectiveness is a jet airplane flying at 600 miles per hour… in the right direction.

Unfortunately, many managers and leaders don't slow down long enough or reflect deeply enough to clarify the right direction. Too many managers have fallen prey to urgency addiction and spend far too little time on activities that are important but not urgent. Too often, the drama of putting out fires promotes the illusion of effectiveness and fuels a vicious cycle of heroics. It stands to reason that if more employees, especially managers, invested more time and energy into proactive, strategic activities, there would be fewer fires to put out in the first place.

But where can managers find the time to be more proactive and strategic when they are already spread thin just tending to all the urgent matters that arise each day and week?

The short answer is that if we can identify activities that are either a waste of time or distractions (from what is truly important), we can reduce the time and attention invested there. The method is fairly simple. You reclaim 1-3 hours, to start, from wasted time, inefficiency or distractions, and re-invest those hours into being proactive (doing things before they become urgent and become a fire that needs putting out).

In the next section, we will introduce a specific framework that we call the "Attention Management Model." This tool will be very helpful for you as you discern reactive activities vs. distractions vs. proactive activities.

The Attention Management Model

This simple framework provides a practical way for leaders to spend less time being reactive or distracted, and to spend more time being proactive.

As we will see, this can significantly reduce stress and boost productivity.

The four "zones" in the illustration represent the primary ways managers spend their time and, more importantly, their attention.

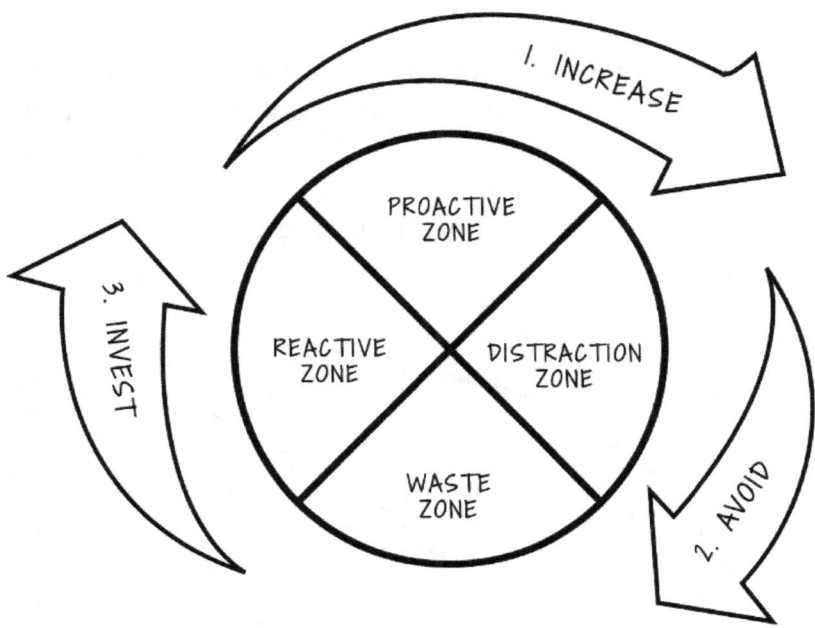

The numbered arrows represent the three fundamental practices that can be used to dramatically enhance productivity while reducing overwhelm and stress.

We will return to this model in a moment, but first, we will review the benefits you can expect from learning and implementing this model.

Once you learn and implement this framework and the specific techniques and practices inherent in it, you can expect:

> To be less reactive.

>To have less time and energy wasted.

> To have fewer interruptions and distractions.

> To be more focused on what's most important.

> To have time, be more strategic and better prepared.

> To enjoy more effective days and weeks.

> To ultimately be more successful in your role as a leader

The "Reactive Zone"

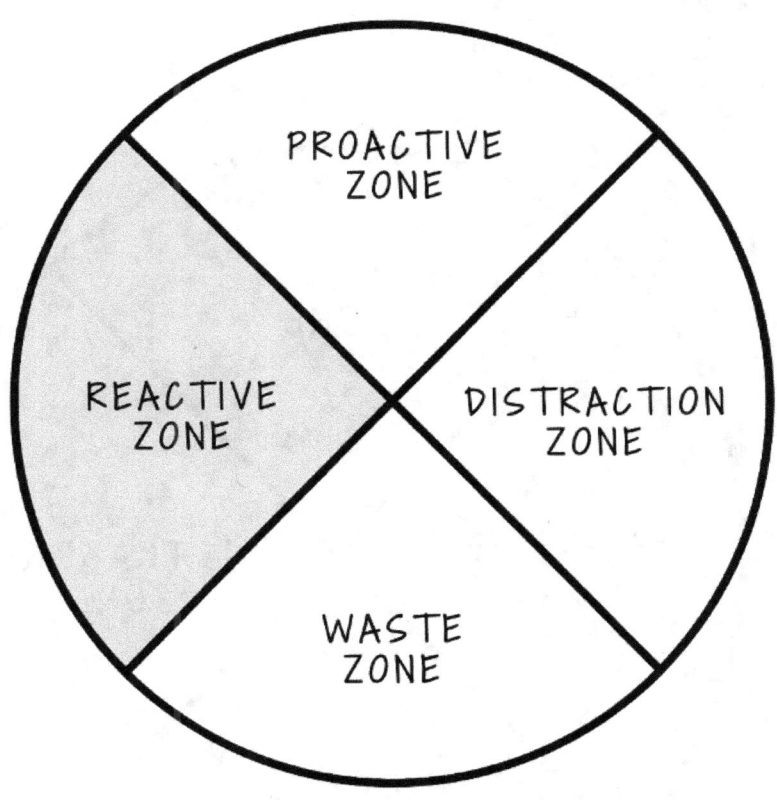

We say they are "important" because they reflect your values and priorities.

You care about them. Naturally, this tends to be the most stressful of the zones.

If you spend much of your time putting out fires or running from deadline to deadline, often behind schedule, then you feel like you have little time for things such as planning, strategic thinking, building reserves, and necessary maintenance.

Keep in mind that the Reactive Zone is not inherently bad; it is necessary to respond to customer and employee needs and demands.

The "Proactive Zone"

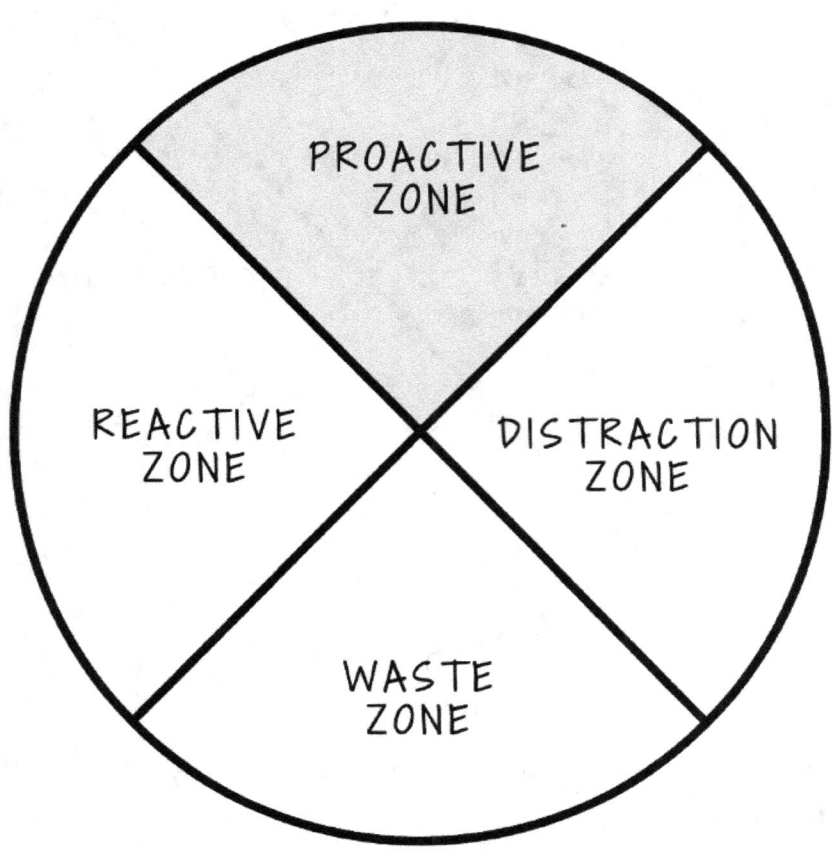

When you are in the *Proactive Zone*, you are focusing your attention on activities (including tasks) that are not urgent, in the sense that they do not have to be done today or even this week. Clearly, there is a lot of value in activities such as strategic thinking, planning, preparation, performing necessary maintenance, and building reserves.

When things are properly maintained, they are less likely to break down and send you spinning into the Reactive Zone. When you take the time for renewal (e.g., breaks, exercise, relaxation, and vacations), you are in a better position to bring your full self to your leadership role and be on your "A Game" when you need to be. Neglecting *Proactive Zone* activities causes the emergencies and crisis situations to just keep coming with greater velocity. This is why so many people find themselves "trapped" in the *Reactive Zone*.

When you spend your day putting out fires, you enjoy the ego gratification of being a hero for the day. A large dose of adrenaline-fueled urgency gives a false feeling of importance.

How can you be more proactive when you already don't have enough time to handle your existing urgent priorities? You might think, "I get it. I'll just stop spending so much time fighting fires in the *Reactive Zone* and spend more time in the *Proactive Zone*".

But here's the catch: You can't just say no to the *Reactive Zone*, because these activities are, in fact, important to you. First, let's clearly define each of these, starting with what I call the "Distraction Zone."

The "Distraction Zone"

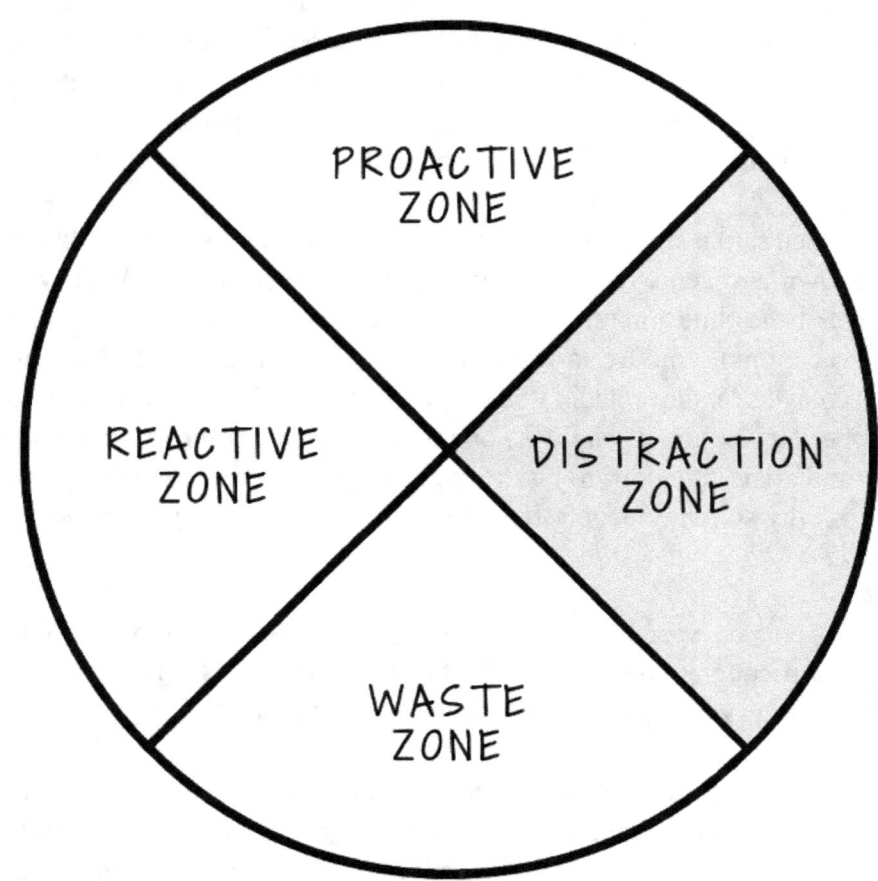

The *Distraction Zone* consists of unnecessary interruptions, distracting calls and emails, and other messages that are not important. As the name implies, this involves activities that distract you from what is truly important to you.

Such activities, or distractions as I am calling them, are considered "time-sensitive" or even "urgent" because they are happening right now in the present moment, grabbing your attention or being "in your face", so to speak. So while they are or at least feel "urgent," they are definitely not "important " in the sense that they are not aligned with your highest priorities or your values.

Note: If they were important, they would not be in this Distraction Zone, they would be in the Reactive Zone where we see activities that are both urgent and important.

While I am saying these activities are not important to you, they might be important to the person interrupting you. This is your "Attention Zone" model, from your perspective, not from theirs.

I estimate that the typical manager spends 5-15 unproductive hours each week having their attention pulled away by these unimportant distractions and interruptions. Imagine if you could reclaim 5-15 hours a week!

What would you do with an extra day of productivity each week?

Could you find some ways to be more successful in your role as a manager?

Why are we as managers so easily distracted, and why do we allow so many interruptions and distractions? It's a good question to ponder.

It might be because we don't value focus and concentration in the first place.

If we don't know the true value of "undivided attention", then we're unlikely to prioritize protecting it. Perhaps we don't set boundaries.

Maybe we fail to block out uninterrupted time each day and each week for ourselves (to work on our key tasks) and guard that time carefully.

Another possible cause is that many managers haven't yet learned to distinguish what is urgent (time-sensitive) from what is important (aligned with their values and priorities).

The techniques and tactics discussed in this session (and other personal productivity hacks) will help you minimize interruptions and distractions.

Next, we will move into the final zone in our model.

The "Waste Zone"

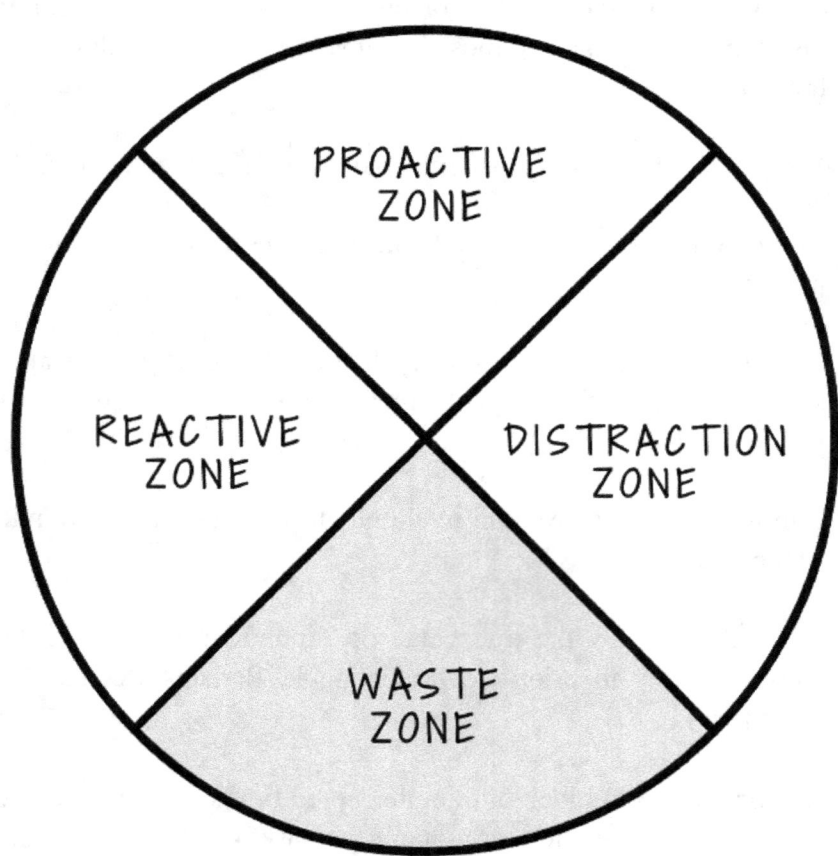

Waste Zone activities are neither urgent nor important—they are simply a waste of time. Workplace productivity research shows that in typical organizations, a tremendous number of hours are spent each week doing meaningless activities that do nothing to advance the organization's goals.

Perhaps the most obvious waste of a manager's time is doing a task for a team member that would be better delegated to that team member (both in terms of productivity and also in terms of skill-building for the employee).

Another *Waste Zone* example is the extra time it takes to complete a task because you were not prepared or properly trained. Consider the executive who still "hunts and pecks" on a keyboard, taking four times longer than necessary to type an email, because he never made the time to take a typing class. Or a manager who spends hours preparing a presentation because she never took the time to take a class or watch some tutorials on PowerPoint or Keynote. Or when meetings or working sessions are much longer than they need to be because no one took the time in advance to create an agenda and gather all the necessary documents.

Another example would be unproductive meetings that are really unnecessary and could easily be replaced with an asynchronous tool such as email or an online dashboard or other status reporting documents. When leaders are not skilled at the practice I call simply, "Running Effective Meetings, then a lot of time (theirs and their employees) are spent in the *Waste Zone*.

A final example would be the time spent searching for paperwork or computer documents that were never properly filed and organized (a proactive activity). When leaders or their teams are disorganized in any way, this causes members to spend more time in this "zone of inefficiency."

The Three Meta-Practices

Now we will walk through the three meta-practices one at a time. These three "practices" are the key to enormous increases in productivity, far less inefficiency and waste, far fewer distractions, and a LOT more time being proactive, making measurable progress toward your most important priorities (and goals) every single week and every month. It is not an overstatement to say that if you implement these three practices, it will change your life. In my experience of teaching these three practices over the past 18 years, I have seen, on average, most executives reclaim about half a day a week (which they then use to focus on their most important goals).

Increase

The first meta-practice is to "increase" awareness of which zone you are in at any given time of the day.

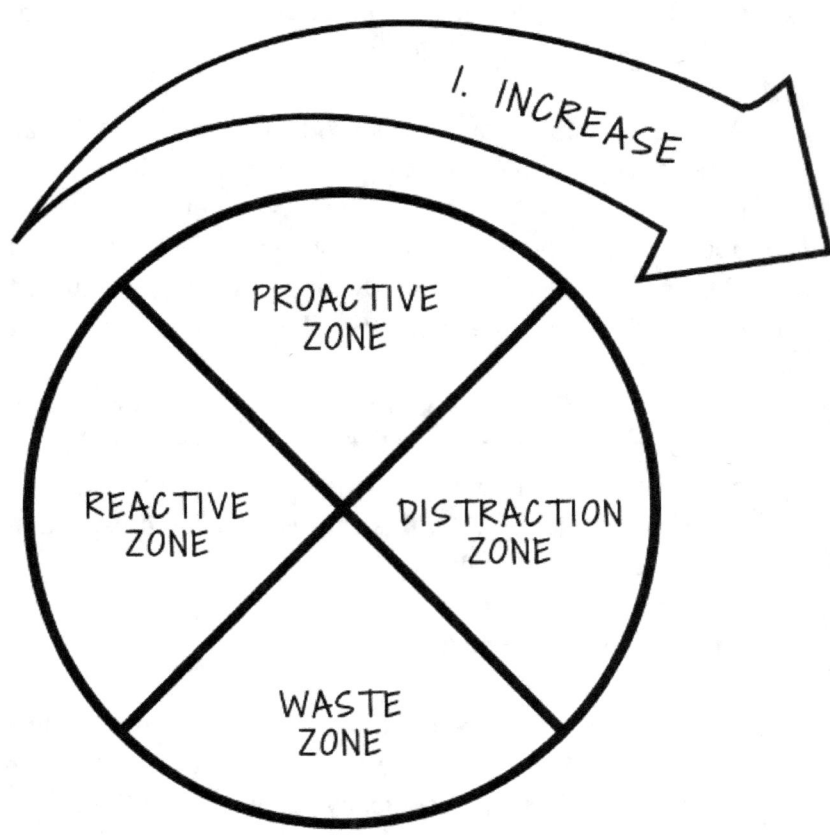

This is, of course, a "mindfulness practice." Get in the habit of being "mindful," of being aware, of noticing and naming the zone you are in every hour of every day. Some leaders log which zone they are in once an hour daily for about a week to help them increase this awareness. If you aren't aware of what zone you are in, then it is hard to improve your productivity or know what you should do to liberate yourself from the "being trapped in the *Reactive Zone*" as I say.

As part of this mindfulness practice, you should ask yourself, "Am I putting out a fire that is both important to you (aligned with your values and key priorities) and also time-sensitive (urgent)?" If yes, you are in the *Reactive Zone*.

Or "Is someone interrupting me with an issue that may be important to them but really isn't on my radar of priorities at all?" If yes, then you are in the *Distraction Zone*.

Avoid

The second meta-practice is to "avoid" distractions and waste. You avoid by asserting your boundaries. You avoid waste by raising your standards.

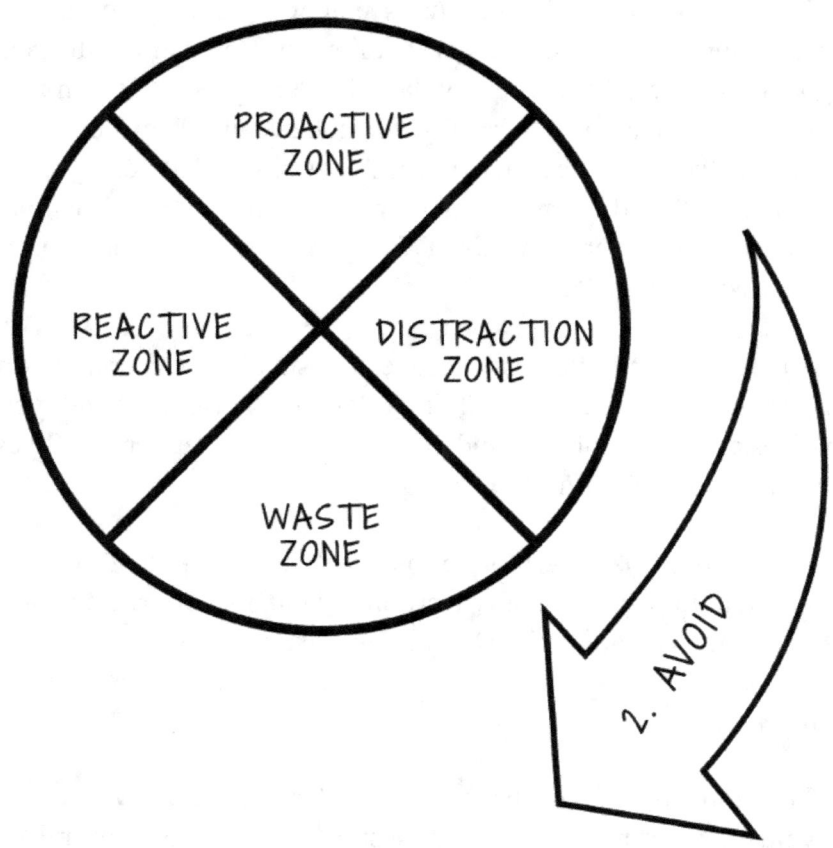

If you are concentrating on completing a time-sensitive deadline, let your coworker know you can't answer his question right now, but you can be available to discuss his project after lunch. You must learn to minimize wasted time and energy by raising your standards.

This means being more organized and prepared for your meetings and your work. It also means choosing to avoid conversations and activities that do not add value (that are not aligned with your values and priorities).

Invest

The third meta-practice is to "invest" the cumulative minutes and hours you have reclaimed from the Distraction and Waste Zones, along with the mental bandwidth and physical energy, into more proactive and more strategic activities.

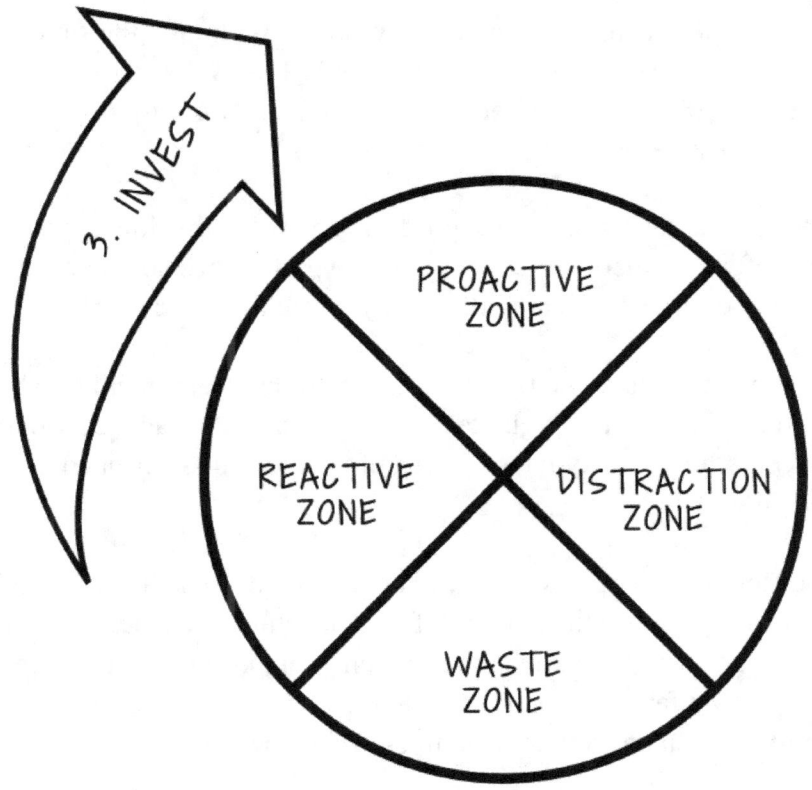

As a leader, your success is not determined by "busy work" or checking off tasks on a task list each week.
A leader's success is determined by her ability to bring successful projects across the finish line each month and each quarter.

Therefore, you must invest a lot of time, energy and mental bandwidth into proactive and strategic tasks and activities each week. Unsophisticated managers allow their email or their urgent tasks to determine where they place their attention.

Sophisticated leaders don't let the, "tail wag the dog". Managers who are excellent at what they do manage their attention very deliberately, strategically and proactively.

An example of this practice of "investing" is to take the time to prepare for next week's meeting agenda this week, so you can share it with your coworkers and get their input on it prior to the day of the meeting.

Another example would be to go ahead and make the time to watch that software video tutorial you've been putting off, so you can be faster and more efficient with a tool you use frequently.

Or you could make the time to speak with that team member who is struggling with a high-stakes project, so you can hear their concerns and offer your support before they miss an upcoming deadline.

The techniques in this section can help you reduce distractions and waste and increase the amount of high-leverage activities you and your team complete each week, each month, and each quarter. After only a few months of application of these methods, it's quite common for managers to reclaim 5-8 hours per week.

It's not uncommon to have a full day of additional productivity within a few months. Imagine getting your pressing (urgent) work done in four days a week, instead of five, and having a whole day to focus on strategic goals that are truly important to you and your organization.

The techniques and tactics discussed in this section and the other personal productivity hacks provided in this chapter will help you level up your own "attention management" significantly.

Like any complex skill, this takes months to master. But you can see an increase in your focus and productivity starting immediately as you begin to deploy these methods.

FOCUS AND CONCENTRATION

In this section, we will be focusing on attention itself.

What do you think focus and concentration are?

How does focus and concentration, or the lack of it, impact your role as a manager in your day-to-day and week-to-week work?

What is your relationship with attention? Is attention something that just goes to whatever stimuli are in your environment? Or are you deliberate about where you put your attention, and for how long?

In your own life and work, you have probably noticed that the times when you have been the most productive often correlate to the times when you were extremely focused and when you were able to bring a strong level of concentration to your work.

But if you're like most people, you might be puzzled by the fact that you can be extremely focused at certain times and completely scattered at others.

Accomplished individuals across multiple disciplines have come to believe that focus and concentration, possibly more than any other factors, are what separates average performers from high performers.

Peak performers are not only in sports and highly technical jobs; they show up in just about every endeavor in life—they work at computers, they run successful meetings, and they have quality relationships with spouses, children, and other loved ones.

Focus, it seems, is a big deal. And judging by popular business magazines and books, it's a growing trend.

Flow Theory is a topic that we introduced in another section. It is highly relevant to focus and concentrate on, so we will mention it again in this section.

The state of flow, also known as the "zone", is the mental state of operation in which a person performing an activity is fully immersed in a feeling of energized focus, full involvement, and enjoyment in the process of the activity. In essence, flow is characterized by complete absorption in what one does and losing a sense of space and time.

We've all felt a sense of flow when we have brought our full focus and concentration to an enjoyable activity: playing sports or a favorite game, creating music, driving, or perhaps a particularly engaging conversation.

There are several predictable effects of getting into a flow state. The first is pleasure. It feels great. The second effect of flow is heightened productivity. The flow state opens vast reservoirs of resourcefulness, creativity, and energy. When people are in flow, their productivity and quality can skyrocket. The third effect is that afterward, when looking back on the experience, people tend to feel a deep sense of satisfaction.

Think about that. When you get into a flow state while working at your job as a manager, you will not only be more productive, but you will likely love the experience of the work itself!

There are four key dynamics that combine to create flow:

1) A balance between challenges and skills, which we discussed in another section.

2) Clear objectives, which we explore in the planning and project management sections of this book.

3) Frequent feedback to know if you're achieving those objectives or not (we discussed this in the learning section of this book)

4) Focus and concentration achieved by minimizing distractions and strengthening the muscle of concentration. This is the main focus of this section.

Interestingly, the workplace can be an ideal place to experience flow when people have the opportunity to be free from distractions and engage in a single activity for a period of time.

Perhaps you've experienced working on a deadline for a proposal or preparing for an important presentation, and you've blocked out two hours for the task.

You were probably surprised at how fast the time flew by, how unstressful it was once you dropped into the mode of full concentration, and how much you enjoyed it. That was the flow.

The problem is, many people are so distracted and don't understand the importance of blocking out an hour or two of time for an important task, they rarely experience this high-performance state.

Concentration is Crucial

Concentration can be defined as the ability to deliberately control where attention is focused and to hold it there for as much time as desired without being distracted by what is not relevant to the task at hand.

One of the most universal of all natural tools, concentration is important for almost every human endeavor. The productivity of just about any activity is enhanced by the ability to concentrate.

The ability to concentrate means that you're in control of where your attention goes, rather than being at the whim of external distractions.

Being able to focus and concentrate does not imply that you cut yourself off from anything important or push anything away.

It simply means that you have the ability to attend to exactly what is appropriate in that moment and withdraw attention from (ignore) that which is not relevant to the activity.

The capacity to concentrate puts you in the driver's seat. To get better at managing your attention, much less getting into a flow state, you need to hone your concentration skills.

The Massive Trend Called Mindfulness

Leaders familiar with the practice of mindfulness are likely aware of its use among elite athletes, martial artists, fighter pilots, and advanced meditators.

Mindfulness, like its cousin flow, is extremely enjoyable and can significantly increase productivity. Whether you are preparing a proposal, responding to an email, having a difficult conversation with a customer or colleague, or delivering a high-stakes presentation, mindfulness enhances performance.

Mindfulness practitioners are more aware of their thoughts, and less reactive to them.

When they experience an emotional reaction (for example, when emotionally triggered), mindfulness practitioners are more able to dispassionately observe that reaction in their mind and body and make a conscious choice about what to do next.

Psychologists call this capacity emotional maturity. Naturally, this is extremely important for managers to be successful in their roles.

Several decades of mindfulness research have convinced numerous corporations to make significant investments into training their employees in the practice.

These include: Google, Aetna, Intel, General Mills, Target, and countless others.

These corporations have found that mindfulness dramatically increases the employees' ability to listen, reflect, make decisions, and produce. The ability to focus and reflect on all available options results in better, more-informed decisions.

Focusing with full attention on important conversations results in a higher quality of interaction and collaboration with colleagues. The attention management practices introduced in this book provide practical ways to bring more mindfulness to your work activities. In a very real sense, attention management tactics are, in fact, mindfulness practices.

The foundation and the key to all of this are your ability to focus and concentrate.

Many sections in this book offer tactics that can help you reduce distractions, assert boundaries, block your time on your calendar, and strengthen your concentration. All of these tactics are good ways to put the principles described in this section to work to help you improve your focus and concentration.

Of all the methods, one of the best ways to strengthen this capacity is what we call "single-tasking" which we will explain in another section. So you will want to put a special emphasis on that practice.

By implementing the principles described in this section, you can strengthen your ability to focus and concentrate and bring your best to your role as a manager and leader.

Single Pointed Concentration

In this section, we will contrast the productivity-enhancing practice of
single-tasking with the disastrous, productivity destroying practice commonly known as multitasking.

There was a time when many people believed multitasking was a valuable job skill. They would even write "good at multitasking" on their resumes. However, more than a hundred reputable studies have been published proving that human multitasking is a myth. Computer chips multitask (that's where the term "multitask" comes from). Human brains do not.

People are either attending to one activity at a time, which we call single-tasking, or they are dividing their attention across two or more activities, which is multitasking.

Naturally, when multitasking, each activity suffers because a human being has one consciousness and one unit of conscious attention to spread across the number of activities with which he or she is engaged.

Sue Shellenbarger wrote in The Wall Street Journal:

"A growing body of scientific research shows that one of the juggler's favorite time-saving techniques, multitasking, can actually make you less efficient and, well, stupider."

She continues, "Trying to do two or three things at once or in quick succession can take longer overall than doing them one at a time, and it tends to leave you with reduced brainpower to perform each task."

Numerous neuroscientists and brain researchers have published their findings about the multitasking myth. MIT neuroscientist Earl Miller—one of the world's experts on divided attention— explains that our brains are simply "not wired to multitask well..." When people think they're multitasking, they're actually just switching from one task to another very rapidly. And every time they do so, there's a cognitive cost in doing so.

Don't ever confuse multitasking—trying to do more than one activity at the same time (meaning in the span of 5-15 minutes)—with managing multiple projects.

All managers, and most employees, have multiple projects and multiple tasks. If you complete one task before going on to another, you can complete dozens of tasks in a day. That is not multitasking.

When you take in more information by having multiple simultaneous "experiences", it may feel like you are doing more or doing it faster. That is an illusion.

Every time you divide your attention, you reduce the amount of intelligence and skill you can bring to each activity. You perform the tasks more slowly and with more errors than if you complete one task before moving to the next.

Of course, not all tasks are equal. The inefficiency of multitasking is most pronounced with activities that require abstract thought and careful attention.

Tasks that can be done in a rote manner using your hands or feet with almost no conscious thought — like walking and chewing gum or brushing your teeth while listening to a podcast recording — see a less pronounced loss in effectiveness.

Multitaskers picture themselves as expert jugglers, astounding their audience by keeping five balls in the air with grace, ease, a smile, and a wink.

In reality, multitaskers are more like unskilled, amateur plate spinners, spinning one plate, then another, then frantically racing from one to the next (ignoring the others) while at any moment one might come crashing down.

The more things you try to juggle at the same time, the less effective you become because of the time and attention lost when mentally switching from one activity to the next.

This concept of "task switching" has become central to researchers' understanding of why multitasking is so disastrous to productivity and performance, especially for managers and executives whose work involves abstract thinking, problem-solving, and decision-making.

Research shows that it takes 20 to 40 percent longer to complete a group of tasks while multitasking — with nearly twice as many errors. Have you ever noticed how stressed and exhausted you feel after multitasking for a few hours? The root cause is cortisol — the stress hormone.

Research shows that multitasking significantly increases the production of cortisol as well as the fight-or-flight hormone adrenaline. This explains, in part, why multitaskers often feel mentally foggy and overwhelmed.

The prefrontal cortex of the brain has a novelty bias. Human attention is easily pulled away by something new (shiny object syndrome). This puts knowledge workers—which include managers and leaders—at a disadvantage.

The abstract thinking part of the brain we most need to do our jobs (focusing, learning, solving problems, and making decisions) is easily distracted.

A text comes in, or we have an idea and quickly open a new tab to do a Google search, or we jot down something we need to do later — each of these indulgences tweaks the novelty – and reward-seeking prefrontal cortex, causing a squirt of dopamine, further reinforcing our delusion that we are good at multitasking.

A study funded by Hewlett-Packard and conducted by the Institute of Psychiatry found that, when multitasking, people show a temporary 10-point drop in their IQ — more than twice that found in studies of the impact on mental performance under the influence of marijuana.

Multitaskers also suffer diminished mental performance similar to that seen in people who get no sleep the night prior to a test. Think of that! Working under the influence of multitasking erodes your performance worse than coming into the office high on THC.

A study conducted by the *Virginia Tech Transportation Institute* and repeated by several other organizations shows that a driver who is texting or reading email is 23 times more likely to have a collision. Multitasking behind the wheel is actually more dangerous than driving drunk.

If multitasking is more dangerous than drunk-driving, it is reasonable to say that multitasking at work is as bad if not worse than drunk-working. Stop doing it!

While studies have been conducted and widely published for two decades about the myth of multitasking, more recent studies about how the brain takes in, stores and processes information and learns new skills is even more astonishing. It turns out that multitasking is absolutely disastrous when trying to learn something.

Stanford neuroscientist Russ Poldrack, found that trying to learn new information while multitasking causes the new information to actually be saved into the wrong part of the brain.

When there are no distractions, the information goes straight into the hippocampus region of the brain, where it is organized and stored for later, easy retrieval.

But when learners are multitasking, the data is routed into the striatum region of the brain, which is best suited for storing procedures, not facts and ideas! This means that the likelihood that the information will be learned correctly, leading to new knowledge and skills, is extremely low. Put simply, multitasking totally sabotages learning.

When you are learning, bring your full, undivided attention, or don't do it at all. Otherwise, you are simply wasting your time. Or worse, learning something wrong!

There is little merit in multitasking at work. Just stop doing it. Try to bring your full, undivided attention to everything you do.

If you do find yourself distracted or trying, like the amateur plate spinner, to do multiple things at work, remember, you are not multitasking. That is impossible. Only computer chips multitask. You are actually divi-tasking. You are simply dividing your attention across two or more activities making you stupider, forgetful and accident prone.

When you are working, organize your calendar so that you can fully concentrate on one thing at a time for at least half an hour at a stretch. If you can block out an hour or two for each activity, you might even surprise yourself by dropping into a flow state and producing some of your best work (with less stress).

Per the focus and concentration and flow sections in this book, bringing your full, undivided attention to an activity will not only result in higher performance, it will also be a lot more enjoyable and less stressful.

Can you recall a time when you were highly focused and effective and delivered impressive results? That was likely a time when you were single-tasking.

You focused on what you were doing, brought your full, undivided attention, and gave 100%. Why not bring that quality of awareness to every important activity?

By implementing the single-tasking guidelines in this section, you will strengthen your ability to focus, concentrate, and get the results you want more easily and more efficiently. It should be obvious that one's ability to focus one's attention, at will, on the activities that are most important is central to effective leadership as well as productivity within your team or organization.

This concludes our discussion on this skill set that I call "Improving Productivity."

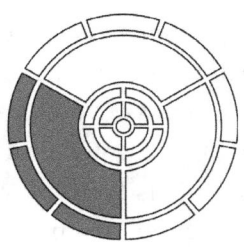

CONCLUSION: WHERE TO GO FROM HERE ON YOUR LEADERSHIP JOURNEY

Congratulations on completing this book. Research studies suggest that less than 50% of non-fiction book buyers actually finish the books they buy. Thank you for your determination to complete this one. Now that you have read this book, you have a strong familiarity with the fundamental leadership abilities and the nine leadership core competencies. You have also learned about numerous frameworks, tools and techniques that fall under the three skill sets we see in the Execution & Performance dimension of leadership. While this is a very positive development, knowledge is not the same as skill. A skill is a "practice" that has been engaged until it becomes a habit. If you want to improve your leadership, then must practice the techniques in this book. Developing the requisite skills described in this book will increase your competency in each of these dimensions. At minimum, you need to adopt and practice these techniques yourself. Experience shows that if you share some of these techniques with your team and invite them to practice these methods with you, as a team, you will learn them faster and your team will benefit from more than one person engaging in it. Socializing these methods (techniques, behaviors) with your team will multiply the benefits for them. As we learned in the section on "deliberate practice," practice doesn't make perfect, rather, perfect practice makes perfect. To increase your competency in these skill sets you have learned about, you must practice the techniques for many weeks (or months). This is the only way to learn a complex skill. You can't learn basketball from a book. You can't learn leadership from a book. But you can learn what you need to do in order to learn these techniques. We have used this method for 20 years helping leaders adopt new skills rapidly with consistent results. You can get the same results if you engage the practices described in this book.

I want to offer you a quick refresher about the principles of deliberate practice that are useful as implement this Accelerating Leadership methodology.

1) *Train technique* - To learn a complex skill, you must isolate the technique or skill, set specific goals based on best practices and benchmarks, practice with full attention and push beyond your comfort zone. You now know how to train.

2) *Rich feedback to calibrate and improve* - This involves practicing the techniques with full attention and effort, and obtaining immediate feedback to be able to calibrate and fine tune the new technique. One way to do this is to share the techniques and practices with your teammates so that they can give you feedback. The best feedback comes from people who have the skill. So, if you have the opportunity to work with coaches or trainers who are familiar with these techniques, that will be ideal. This leads to the next key.

3) *You must get expert mentorship* – I have been able to provide an initial level of mentorship by describing these techniques. That is an excellent start, and if you are very disciplined and diligent in practicing the methods as described, you can make some progress. However, mastery of these techniques, especially the more

complex ones, requires getting individualized feedback and coaching from people who have legitimate expertise (who are experts in the specific techniques). Some of your coaches, advisors or trainers may be legitimate experts in one or more of these techniques (listening, giving feedback, project management). Take advantage of that.

Here's how to apply this knowledge to your situation:

1. Assess your current leadership approach – Identify your dominant leadership style and evaluate where you need to expand your versatility.
2. Develop your leadership skills deliberately – Focus on practicing specific leadership techniques using the deliberate practice framework outlined in this book.
3. Adapt to different followers and contexts – Use the Leadership Rosetta Stone to recognize the worldviews of those you lead and adjust your leadership approach accordingly.
4. Commit to ongoing growth – Leadership is not a one-time event; it is a continuous process of learning, refining, and improving.
5. Attend a course or coaching program where you can receive expert guidance and ongoing feedback to help you internalize the skills efficiently.

To increase your competency in these skill sets you have learned about, you must practice the techniques for many weeks (or months). This is the only way to learn a complex skill. To put this method into practice, active and ongoing training in the specific techniques is required. That is best done in a training and/or coaching environment. My partners and I, across numerous institutes and academies, offer numerous Integral Leadership training and coaching programs in various formats and at various price points to be able to accommodate most leaders in most circumstances. If you are serious about becoming a more effective leader, or if you support leaders (as a trainer or coach), I hope that you will pick up and read one or more of my other (longer, more detailed) books on this subject. You can find all of my books on Amazon.com. I also hope you will consider joining one of the many Integral Leadership training and coaching programs that my partners and I offer. My fourteen books are used as textbooks at multiple institutions and academies and offer various versions of my Integral Leadership training by several different names, including the Integral Leadership Program (many versions across several academies), the Integral Leadership MBA, the Executive Leadership Program and the C-Suite Leadership Program. When you participate in an in-depth online or in-person training based on this content, and especially if you obtain group or one-on-one coaching from a coach who has been trained in my content, then you will be able to rapidly accelerate your development as a leader, and ultimately become the kind of respected influential, impactful, successful leader you know that you are destined to be.

I look forward to continuing this "conversation" with you in one of my other books.

Brett Thomas

ABOUT THE AUTHOR

Leadership authority Brett Thomas is an expert on leadership development, integral theory, and developmental psychology. He has written 14 books on management and leadership. In collaboration with Ken Wilber, he created the world's first "unifying theory of leadership" and wove together 100 years of leadership theory into a unified model that explains which theories and approaches will work with which people and circumstances that also accurately predicts which leadership styles and approaches will be disastrous failures with which specific types of people and circumstances. He is the creator (along with his mentor Ken Wilber) of the popular practice known as Integral Leadership. Brett's fourteen books are used as textbooks around the world in many of the top leadership training and coaching programs. Numerous institutions and academies teach various versions of Brett's highly respected Integral Leadership Program, sometimes using other names such as the Executive Leadership Program, the C-Suite Leadership Program, and the Integral Leadership MBA. Brett is a serial entrepreneur and leader working behind the scenes in more than a dozen humanitarian efforts under the umbrella of the international non-profit (501c3) he quietly founded years ago. Brett is the mentor, advisor, and coach to hundreds of CEOs. Dozens of his clients have scaled their companies from tens of millions to hundreds of millions in revenue and even to over a billion in some cases (while going from dozens to hundreds to thousands of employees), always with a "balanced scorecard" and "triple bottom line," meaning a rich, healthy, beloved culture never merely profit-seeking. In addition to writing books, Brett serves as an advisor to dozens of CEOs and C-Suite Executive Teams, serves as a fractional COO to several organizations, and teaches in several academies. In addition to co-founding two of the most respected and admired leadership academies in the world, he is also one of the primary co-founders of the Conscious Capitalism movement, which he helped launch nearly two decades ago to make "business a force for good.

OTHER BOOKS BY BRETT THOMAS

Integral Leadership: The World's First Unifying Theory of Leadership That Will Forever Change How You Understand, Practice and Develop Leadership

Reinventing Leadership: Discover the Revolutionary Method That Thousands of Leaders and Organizations Are Using to Rapidly Improve Leadership Performance and Organizational Results

Blowing the Whistle on Bogus Leadership: Veteran Industry Insider Reveals Why the Leadership Development Industry is Not Developing Leaders.

The Leadership Rosetta Stone: Discover Which Leadership Approaches Will Work With Which People and Circumstances and Which Approaches Will Be Disastrous Failures with Which People and Circumstances

The Universal Leadership Model: Simplicity on the Other Side of Complexity

Worldviews: The Four Mindsets That Determine What People Perceive, Believe and Value, and Which Leadership Styles They Will Follow

Leadership Styles: How to Be a More Respected, More Influential and More Impactful Leader Using the Right Leadership Style With the Right People and Circumstances

Leadership Intelligence: Learn How Your Cognitive, Emotional, Social and Moral Development is Impacting Your Leadership Performance and How Leaders Can Now Benchmark and Boost These Intelligences

Accelerating Leadership: The Groundbreaking Method for Rapid Leadership Skill Development That Achieves Twice the Results in Half the Time at a Fraction of the Cost

Strategy & Alignment: How the Most Successful Leaders Analyze Needs, Find Leverage, Craft Vision, Align Stakeholders and Create Smart, Strategic Plans

Teamwork & Culture: How the Most Successful Leaders Create the Container, Communicate Effectively, and Consistently Keep Everyone Engaged and Motivated

Execution & Performance: How the Most Successful Leaders Close Expectation Gaps, Maintain High Accountability and Productivity, and Reliably Deliver Excellent Results

Academic Books:

Handbook of Leadership Development: The Definitive Guide for Executives in Charge of Leadership Development

Leadership Psychology: How to Apply Crucial Insights from Positive Psychology, Developmental Psychology, Integral Psychology and Organizational Psychology to Develop More Effective Leaders   (To be published in 2025)

www.ingramcontent.com/pod-product-compliance
Lightning Source LLC
Chambersburg PA
CBHW052148220526
45471CB00004B/1573